THE WAY OF FREEDOM

Understanding Biblical Theology for the
Twenty-First Century Church

Robert Samuel Thorpe

"Stand fast therefore in the liberty wherewith Christ
hath made us free . . . " Galatians 5:1

Copley Custom Textbooks
An imprint of XanEdu Publishing, Inc.

ISBN 13: 978-1-58152-731-5
ISBN 10: 1-51852-731-4

Scripture quotations are from the King James Authorized Version of 1611 with occasional personal modifications for clearer renderings.

Copley Custom Textbooks
An imprint of XanEdu Publishing, Inc.
138 Great Road
Acton, Massachusetts 01720
800-562-2147

For Chrissy, the love of my life
And for all my children, Anna, James, John, and Ben and
their spouses and children, all the most wonderful
people in the world

Table of Contents

Introduction

The Way of Freedom
Understanding Biblical Theology for the 21st Century Church

INTRODUCTION

The post-modern Christian Church is afflicted by an insidious theology that places the responsibility for all the activities and actions in the world on the shoulders of individual Christians. This theology requires people to do all kinds of spiritual gymnastics in order to get God to bless them. First, Christians have to speak the 'right' things in certain 'right' ways to defeat the demons of hell who are destroying churches. Secondly, they have to use the proper formulas of rituals and biblical passages to bring about healings of the sick and salvation for the lost. Finally Christians must work hard to evangelize everyone quickly to take over the world for God before too many people die and go to hell. This theology is complete rubbish and totally non-biblical.

We have not taught Christians to read the Bible and understand theology. So they have concocted a "make-it-happen" theology that promises control of life and the achievement of "success" in the post-modern world. Christians are living in a fantasy world of make believe. They are doing useless things, affecting no one and nothing, pretending to be involved in some high-powered spiritual realm, conquering something that isn't there. It is a life of bondage and failure, a denial of reality, an ignorance of truth, a set-up for complete defeat.

Even when this system is an obvious failure, Christians blame themselves. "I don't have enough faith," they cry or are told by their equally ineffective pastors. So we just try harder, quote more Scripture, pray more, fast more, cry and wail for God to come do what we want, all to no avail. What is needed is a clear understanding of biblical theology, a way of freedom and rest, not working harder in the flesh.

Christianity is not magic; we don't wave magic wands over problems and expect them to disappear. We need to realize the truth and understand the ways of God, which will set us free from condemnation, failures, ineffectiveness, fruitlessness, and weakness. The way of freedom can be seen throughout the Bible, but we shall study passages with which we are familiar but don't realize the depth of truth in them. I pray the Lord will enlighten and free all readers from their well-intentioned, but misguided bondages to live in peace and freedom.

CHAPTER ONE
The Nature of God

We do *not* get doctrine first from the Scriptures. So many people look to the Bible to find doctrines and performance formulas, like a user manual, but in so doing we have missed the major point of the Book. Usually we start our Christian walk with performance-based religious actions; do this and do that. Then by doing these things, we learn the "doctrines of the Bible" which are meant to make us more informed about our "religion." Then we think we know God better and understand the Bible. WRONG ! !

First we must learn the nature of God. That's the primary function of the Bible, to *reveal* the nature of God. That's what revelation is – revealing something. In the case of the Scriptures, the revelation is of God, who He is, what kind of Being He is, what He wants, what He likes, how He thinks, what He does. *Secondly,* once we understand these things and know what kind of God we have relationship with, we then can understand His instruction and His wisdom. *Finally*, then we will understand doctrine and Christian living. Look *first* for pictures of Him in every biblical passage, *then* get the complete picture of Him and know Him as He has chosen to reveal Himself to us. For examples, let's practice recognizing His nature with some typical biblical passages.

God is the Creator -- "**In the beginning God created the heavens and the earth" (Genesis 1:1).**

The word "created" (bara' in Hebrew) means "brought into existence from nothing," which means that God did not use existing materials to fashion the universe but rather created it by His word from nothing. Everything that exists owes its existence to His gift of creation (see John 1:3; Colossians 1:16). There is no force or being called Nature that gradually brought life into existence through random evolution. There was nothing but God and He created. He is the only answer to the basic question of life. "Why is there something rather than nothing?" There is something because He willed it and caused it to exist.

"Let there be lights" in verse 14 means the sun, moon, and stars "in the skies" to be for the computation and recognition of time and seasons. These "lights" are types of "the Light" from 1:3, the cosmic energy of the universe. This is the beginning of time, as we understand it. Note, then, that God is beyond time. He is always "now" which is why we think of Him as always "was" and always "shall be." Technically the only verb tense that correctly describes God's time is "NOW."

The purpose of the "lights" that rule the sky is to "give light upon the earth." Modern science fiction and Darwinian science have made the notion of life on other planets very attractive and popular but such ideas are manifestly untrue. Though there are myriads of stars, constellations, galaxies, and planets, the only sentient life in the universe is on this earth, which is the focus of God's love and activity of salvation. The abundance of celestial bodies is part of the idea of the extravagance of God.

It's all there to show us His magnificence and His care for us. We don't need the tremendous diversity of colors, shapes, sizes, and textures of flowers, trees, sunsets, and other beauty in the universe for life to exist. The clam doesn't know that the inside of his shell is brilliant purple, silver, blue, and pink but we know because God made it for us to see. Beauty is the idea of God and He allowed us to recognize it. But it is God's pleasure to make the earth this way, so that we might enjoy the place He made for us and recognize His majesty and greatness. The same is said for the stars and planets.

Just from the text of Genesis 1, we realize many things about God. He is omnipotent, which means that He can do whatever He needs or wants to do. He has all power. "Power" means the ability to make something happen. All things with power in the universe derive that power from God. All things that exist derive that existence from God, who is the only self-existent Being. There is no other power in the universe, heaven, or earth that is remotely comparable to the power of God. He simply spoke and the universe appeared. There are no other gods; the devil has no power but what is given to him, and no other being, not even you, is powerful enough to stop or hinder God from doing what He determines should be done. So we are not talking about a God who has difficulty making things happen. We are not talking about a God who must depend on anything or anyone to make things happen. He is not waiting for you to pray or fast or do anything before He does what He wills to do. He does not need anything or anyone. He is not lonely. He does not need us to preach or pray for the sick or anything else, but . . . He chooses to share His life, His ministry, His works, with us. He wants us to be a part of what He does, like parents with children. It's all about relationship. Everything about life involves our relationship with God.

He is trustworthy and infinitely capable. He has given us grace (John 1:14), which is "undeserved favor."

He likes us and wants to bless us, extravagantly, abundantly. So God can handle any problem you've got, without your help, thank you very much. So why don't we trust Him completely? He wants to give us real life, not have us reform our old broken lives. We can't rescue ourselves, but He rescues us through Christ, not through our religious rituals or self-righteousness. Life is about Him; the whole Bible is about Him.

There are many verses that describe the creation such as **Isaiah 45:12-18 "I have made the earth and created man upon it. I, even my hands, have stretched out the heavens (***heavens*** means everything** we see in the sky), **and all their hosts have I commanded. For thus saith the LORD that created the heavens, God Himself that formed the earth and made it, He hath established it, He created it not in vain, He formed it to be inhabited..."**

Clearly the LORD created the universe and the earth for us, to be our home, for us to live on in fellowship with Him. There is no random accident here, but purpose and intent. We should be good stewards of this home He built us, which is so well done that, even in its fallen state, the ecosystems, the seasons, the animal kingdom, and all its processes still work so beautifully together. But the bottom line is that He made it all, designed it and built it Himself, and keeps it going (Heb. 1).

"Thou even thou, art LORD alone; thou hast made heaven, the heaven of heavens, with all their hosts (all the stars and planets), the earth and all things that are therein, the seas and all that is therein, and thou preservest them all..." (Nehemiah 9:5-6, 17, 31-32).

Again there are no gods but Him. Nothing else in the universe, in the sky, in the earth, or anywhere else, is divine. He alone is God. He made everything and is the owner of it all. Therefore everything and everyone is accountable to Him. No one is autonomous; no one is innocent; no one exists without His consent. As well, God "preserves" the universe. This is the definition of the old word "Providence;" which means that God takes care of the universe. He upholds it all with the word of His power (Hebrews 1:3).

"God, that made the world and all things therein, seeing that He is Lord of heaven and earth, dwelleth not in temples made with hands, neither is worshipped with men's hands, as though He needed anything, seeing He giveth to all life, and breath, and all things..." (Acts 17:24-29).

God has no needs; He doesn't need me or you but He chooses to have relationship with us. He chose to create; He chose to make all things the way He did. All existence comes from Him, He who is the self-existent, uncreated eternal Being. But things on earth and the universe are the way they are because it was His choice to make them that way, such things as gender, morality, days and nights, sleep, species reproduction, color, and so on. Perhaps if we thought about this idea a little more, we may begin to look at these things differently. Sex is a gift and choice of God, not an act to simply fulfill some animal instinct in us. Sleep is a necessary thing for us, as is rest, so that the bodies we have been given will be healthy. Gender is the choice of God, that some of us are female and some male. To deny this concept or try to diminish the importance of one gender or the other is clearly a rebellious action. Morality is not simply a social choice but a divine imperative, and He knows which moral choices are best for us. His ways are always the best ways.

"I am He, I am the first and I also am the last. Mine hand also hath laid the foundation of the earth and my right hand hath spanned the heavens. When I call unto them, they stand up together" (Isaiah 48:12-15). God has complete and total authority and power over all the elements of the universe. He is the ultimate Being in the universe. All the universe obeys His commands.

"Who hath ascended up into heaven, or descended? Who hath gathered the wind in His fists? Who hath bound the waters in a garment? Who hath established all the ends of the earth?" (Proverbs 30:4). Obviously, only God, and certainly no man. Clearly, the wind, the waters, and the ends of the earth all belong to God, since He made them.

"Where wast thou (Job) when I (God) laid the foundations of the earth? Who hath laid the measures thereof? ...Who laid the cornerstone thereof?" (Job 38: 4-39:30). God, not man, did all these things.

"Bless the Lord, O my soul, O LORD my God, thou art very great; Thou art clothed with honor and majesty; who coverest thyself with light as with a garment; who stretchest out the heavens like a curtain.." (Psalm 104:1-35).

This most interesting passage pictures the sky as a curtain that God has erected. From this scene we can begin to conceive that God is much bigger and greater than the universe. As well, the psalmist describes the vision of God in light, that God covers Himself with light.

This light is also greater than the light of the universe; stronger than all electromagnetic energy from which stars are made, yet only God uses it as a cloak. Such energy could make all the stars in the universe evaporate, yet has no effect on the being of God. Such greatness we cannot pretend to comprehend.

God is Eternal -- **"And God said to Moses, 'I AM THAT I AM' (Exodus 3:14).**

The notion of eternity conjures many different pictures in our minds. We think of extremely long periods of time. "When we've been there ten thousand years, ..." exclaims one famous hymn of the Church, which signifies this idea of long time. However, God is greater than time. He is present in time *and* beyond time. He created time. "But beloved, be not ignorant of this one thing, that one day is with the LORD as a thousand years and a thousand years as one day" (2 Peter 3:8). Peter's comment indicates that time does not affect God. There is no such thing as "before God was," since He *is* (see John 8:58)]. There was no history before God. He has always been, rather He always is. He is always NOW. Eternity is a forever NOW. We won't be counting days in eternity (see Revelation 21:22-26). So the gift of God to us, eternal life (Romans 6:23) in Christ Jesus, is continued existence forever, in an unending NOW and not only eternal but abundant in joy, peace, and righteousness – no pain, no death, no sorrow, no evil of any kind (Revelation 21:3-8; Romans 14:17).

God is Omnipresent -- **"Thou compassest [surround] my path, and my lying down. ...Thou hast beset [set yourself around] me behind and before and laid thine hand upon me... Whither shall I go from thy spirit, or whither shall I flee from thy presence? If I ascend up into heaven, thou art there; if I make my**

bed in hell [Sheol, the place of the shades, the place of the dead], behold thou art there. If I take the wings of the morning and dwell in the uttermost parts of the sea, even there shall thy hand lead me, and thy right hand shall hold me" (Psa.139:3-10).

God is everywhere. That does not mean that everything is God. It means that His presence fills all the creation. In some way, He is always here, with us. The word Immanuel means "God with us." Solomon said **"But will God indeed dwell on the earth? Behold, the heaven and heaven of heavens cannot contain Thee; how much less this house that I have builded?" (1 Kings 8:27; 2 Chronicles 2:6; Acts 7:48-49).** How much less indeed! God is greater than all His creation. **"Am I a God at hand, saith the Lord, and not a God afar off? Can any hide himself in secret places that I shall not see him, saith the LORD? Do not I fill heaven and earth, saith the Lord?"(Jeremiah 23:23-24).** No one escapes the sight of God. He knows all the actions and thoughts of all people.

The Apostle Paul further explains this notion to the Athenians in Acts 17, **"God that made the world and all things therein, seeing that He is Lord of heaven and earth, dwelleth not in temples made with hands; ...that they should seek the Lord, if haply [perhaps] they might feel after Him and find Him, though He be not far from every one of us. For in Him we live and move and have our being" (Acts 17:24-28).** We cannot in a literal, concrete sense, get "closer to God" than we already are. We can be better aware of Him, feel that our relationship is more intimate and vital, and sense His presence wherever we go but physically and locationally, we are "in Christ," living in God, acting and thinking with His Being right there where we are, always. Hence it makes no sense to literally "invite" Jesus to come into our worship services or ask the Holy Spirit to "come down" and fill the church building.

These are figures of our speech, accommodation by God to our limited comprehension. He is already wherever we are. No matter where you are or what your situation is, God is there, to cry or laugh with you, to comfort and console, to chastise if necessary and encourage you. He will never leave you, for any reason.

"For I am persuaded that neither death nor life, nor angel nor principalities nor powers, nor things present nor things to come, nor height nor depth, nor any other creature shall be able to separate us from the love of God which is in Christ Jesus our Lord" (Romans 8: 38-39); ". . . for He hath said, I will never leave thee nor forsake thee" [which literally reads in Greek, "By no means will I leave thee nor by no means will I forsake thee"]**(Hebrews 13:5).**

God spoke to Joshua after the death of Moses that ". . . as I was with Moses, so will I be with thee. I will not fail [leave] thee nor forsake thee" (Joshua 1:5). In Joshua's renewal of God's covenant with Israel after they had settled in Canaan, he states twice that ". . . the Lord thy God, he it is that doth go with thee. He will not fail [leave] thee nor forsake thee" (Deuteronomy 31:6-8). How much more will He stay with us, His children in Christ, hence the emphatic promise in Hebrews 13:5? (See Deuteronomy 4:39; Isa. 57:15; 66:1). There's no need for us to try to hunt for God, or to ask Him to come to us or to a particular place or to think that He is so "out there" that He is not also "right here."

The term "presence of God" is like the illustration of a person coming to see the king and being allowed into the presence of the king. It's more of a formal awareness of where we are and where the king is; that we are in close proximity. But God, unlike the king, is not limited to one location, such as in the palace. He is already everywhere; we simply need to be aware of Him and realize that we are in His formal presence all the time. As such, we should be aware that He sees all of our failings and successes, that we can hide nothing from Him, and that He is ready to help us instantly. He is in us and around us and with us all at once.

God is Righteous -- **"The Lord our God is righteous in all His works which He doeth" (Daniel 9:14).**

The best definition of Righteous is "the right character of God." He is right, holy, sinless. "Righteous are thee, O Lord" (Jeremiah 12:1). We would not know what righteousness means if not for the definition of God that informs us that His character and actions are right, hence righteous. Those attitudes and actions which reflect His are right; those which do not reflect His are wrong. Christians, redeemed from sin and regenerated by the Holy Spirit, are made righteous *in Christ.* Our relationship with God, and our standing with Him, is right, i.e. righteous. We are now called righteous because of Christ who is God, sinless and righteous by definition. Our relationship with God is based on the righteousness of Jesus. Even if we fail and sin, we are still righteous in His eyes because of the righteousness of Christ and we are "in Him."

God is Self-Existent -- **"God that made the world and all things therein, seeing that He is Lord of heaven and earth, dwelleth not in temples made with hands; neither is worshipped with men's hands, as though He needed anything, seeing He giveth to all life and breath and all things" (Acts 17:24).**

All beings owe their existence to some source. God is the Source of all life and being. He is the only self-existent Being, who gives existence to all creatures. Nothing in the physical universe can create itself. One of the irrefutable "laws" of science is that something cannot come from nothing. God is the necessary Being, self-existent, and giver of all existence.

Be sure to note that some things we think of as objects or things, are not. Love, joy, peace, evil, good, salvation, sanctification, justification, glorification, etc. etc, are NOT things (objects) and therefore they are not able to be "possessed" by us. We do not have an object, a thing, called love. Love is an attitude and action, not a thing to possess and impart. Neither are the other nouns mentioned earlier. We tend to think of nouns as objects but that is not always the case, especially in theology. We "say" we *have* peace when we feel an absence of anxiety or agitation but we do not have an object called "peace" that we possess and can impart to others.

The same is true of these theological terms. Salvation means rescue. You cannot possess a rescue. It is an attitude and action of God. Sanctification is the same. You do not possess an object called sanctification. The word "sanctification" means "set apart from something, to something else." Hence we are set apart from the world and sin to God. It does not mean literal sinlessness. There is no process of gradually becoming less sinful. In Christ, we are no longer sinful; we are called saints (the holy ones) and our eternal sanctification is in Christ. In John 17:17, God sanctifies us through truth, and we are sanctified wholly by God (I Thessalonians 5:23). We are sanctified by the blood of Christ (Hebrews 13:12). We have already been sanctified by the Holy Spirit in Christ (1 Corinthians 1: 2; 6:11). We are justified in Christ by His grace (Romans 3:24).

In short, in Christ everything is done. We have received everything we need, all spiritual blessings in Christ (Ephesians 1: 3) and we have everything necessary for life and godliness through the knowledge of Christ (2 Peter 1:3). We say "our" existence because we exist as individual beings, but existence is not an object we possess. We exist; our person exists; we experience life and we know we are alive and in a certain place. But we do not possess an object called existence.

"...the everlasting God, ...God only wise..." (Romans 16:25-27). God is the only Being who can give existence, who has always been. There has never been a time when He wasn't. He made time; He is above and beyond time. He is always "now," and always will be.

"Now to the King, eternal, immortal, invisible, the only wise God, be honor and glory forever and ever" (1 Timothy 1:17). His greatness can only be suggested in limited terms like eternal, immortal, honor, and glory forever. Even so, we cannot come close to understanding His greatness.

God is Omnipotent -- **"O Lord God, thou hast begun to show thy servant thy greatness and thy mighty hand; for what God is there in heaven or in earth that can do according to thy works and according to thy might?" (Deuteronomy 3:24).**

To discuss omnipotence, we first understand the word itself; "omni" meaning "over everything, or above all" and "potence" meaning "power," which means then "power over everything or the greatest power conceivable." The word does not mean "power to do anything." God does not have the power to do things that are absurd, such as make Himself non-existent, nor does He have power to do things that contradict His essence, such as make Himself sinful, or do evil, nor can He do things that are impossible by definition, such as make green be red, or make Himself not God. He has power over everything and power greater than any other power. There is no power comparable to His; no one and no thing is even remotely comparable in power. He made the universe with just a few words. Notice the creation described in Genesis 1.

"...and what is the exceeding greatness of His power toward us who believe, according to the working of His mighty power, which He wrought in Christ..." (Ephesians 1:17-21).

God's power, the Holy Spirit, dwells in us and works in us. The full power of the creator God, the omnipotent God, works in us. How can we not be confident and full of faith that He will work on our behalf? We must accept what He does and not get disturbed if He does things differently than what we wanted or expected. But we expect Him to help us and always do what is best for us; more than we ask or think.

"Oh, the depth of the riches both of the wisdom and knowledge of God! How unsearchable are His judgments and His ways past finding out! ...For of Him and through Him and to Him are all things, to whom be glory forever" (Romans 11:33-36).

Paul experienced a loss for words to describe the greatness of God. We can hear the exclamation, the emotion, the overwhelming awe in Paul's heart as he tries to tell us more about God's greatness. The depths are unreachable; the decisions and wisdom of God are beyond any knowledge of ours. Everything is His and He is full of glory and honor.

God is Spirit -- **"God is spirit, and they that worship Him must worship Him in spirit and in truth" (John 4:24).**

God is spirit, purely spirit, which distinguishes Him from human flesh, animals, stars, or other objects in creation. Angels and evil spirits are also spirits (Hebrews 1:7, 14) with one huge difference. They are created beings, subject to God who created them. He is the necessary Being, the one being who is timeless and does not owe His existence to any other being. All created beings, angels or otherwise, owe their existence to Him.

Because of an inadequacy in our English language as well as the influence of TV and film, we tend to consider 'spirit' as a formless, shapeless, unearthly mass or fluid-like substance, similar to the green mist featured in the film, 'The Ten Commandments', which flows along the ground, killing first-born Egyptians. Even the English dictionaries use terms like "incorporeal, immaterial, or principle of power" to help define the notion of spirit. Then we think of a ghost, a being without substance, floating through walls and doors of buildings, and so on. These images do not help our understanding of God. He is a Person, with thought, emotion, and distinction. A spirit may be invisible to human eyes but not necessarily without shape and form and substance. Spirit is a substance, not visible to us, and spirits have shape and form, sometimes made visible to us, such as Gabriel in Luke 1:11 to Zacharias, 1:26 to Mary, 2:9-14 to the shepherds, Matthew 1:20 and 2:13 to Joseph, Matthew 4:11 to Jesus, many times in the Book of Revelation, and in many instances in the Old Testament such as Ezekiel 1 and Daniel 10ff. God is not human, nor does He have a physical body like humans, but He does have shape and form, though not restricted by time or location. He is infinite in every aspect of Himself.

I know this idea is impossible for humans to conceive because we are limited by space, time, location, three dimensions, and physicality. But God is not limited except by His very nature, such that He cannot lie (Hebrews 6:18) or sin or anything else that is contrary to His being and nature. Since He is this way, He will never tell us anything that is untrue. He will always do the best for us. He always does good to us. The word "spirit" both in Hebrew and Greek means "life principle, the thing that makes a being or thing live, enthusiasm, attitude, soul, inner aspect of a living being that makes the being live." Therefore we realize that God's nature is life itself, though life is not God. There is no death in God. Because we are in Christ, we are in life eternal. Because the Holy Spirit dwells in us, we have life permanently and eternally, and nothing can remove this living nature we have received (Romans 8:38-39).

God is Perfect -- "Be ye therefore perfect, even as your Father which is in heaven is perfect" (Matthew 5:48).

We define the notion of "perfect" by the Being of God Himself. He is the standard by which we conceive of "perfect," meaning "fully or thoroughly or completely" the way a thing is meant to be. In Scripture, "perfect" normally means "complete." So that when Noah and Job are called perfect (Genesis 6:9; Job 1:1), the meaning is "complete, doing their best to not live in evil sinful ways." But they were still human, subject to a sinful nature, not sinless. Only Jesus was sinless. Thus completeness and acting according to being, fully as we should be, is the expectation, not sinlessness. And we are only complete in Christ (Colossians 2:10), so He is the way for us to become complete or perfect. God is sinless, since sin is an offense against the person and nature and law of God, and He cannot be nor do anything contrary to His very nature.

"The law of the LORD is perfect, converting the soul; the testimony of the LORD is sure, making wise the simple. The statutes of the LORD are right, rejoicing the heart; the commandment of the LORD is pure, enlightening the eyes..."(Psalm 19:7-11).

Too many people today question the law of God. As well, some people refuse to recognize or obey His law. Yet the Scripture tells us that His law is perfect, sure, right, and pure. We cannot obtain any better laws. Since God made everything, He already knows our needs and the best ways to live in the earth. Why wouldn't we acknowledge that and do what He says? We can't do any better, yet we still try to do our own selfish wills. Stupid, yes?

From the passage here in Psalm 19, we can see some of the benefits provided by the laws of God: restoration of the soul (the inner person), surety or certainty, wisdom, joy, purity (escape from worldliness and the stain of sin), and enlightenment, the awareness of reality and truth. God's laws reflect His nature, which tells us more about Him. He does not allow us to escape from the punishing consequences of sin, except in Christ. His laws and commandments, if followed, would make the world safe, secure, joyful, pure, and enlightened.

"Wilt thou also disannul My judgment? Wilt thou condemn Me that thou mayest be righteous? Hast thou an arm like God?"(Job 40:8-14). Can any being stop the will of God, or thwart His will or challenge His purpose? Nothing and no one can stop God from fulfilling His will and purpose, not even your own sin, which Christ has borne for us, so that we may receive the grace and blessing of God.

"So then it is not of him that willeth nor of him that runneth, but of God that showeth mercy" (Romans 9:10-24). We cannot make ourselves worthy of forgiveness and salvation. We cannot will ourselves to be children of God nor can we work hard enough to earn His favor. It is only through the mercy and grace of God that any person can be rescued from sin and darkness. Salvation is <u>His</u> attitude and action, not ours.

"Thou wilt say then unto me, why doth He yet find fault? For who hath resisted His will? Nay but, O man, who art thou that replieth against God? Shall the thing formed say to Him that formed it, 'why hast thou made me thus?' Hath not the potter power over the clay...?" (Romans 9:19-23).

No one can find fault in God and no one can resist His will; we are His workmanship, not our own. He will do what He wants to do; nothing can stop Him. Perhaps in America, where we have so many choices, the idea that God can do whatever He wants with us, is unsettling. But He is the King, the Lord, the Master, the Absolute Ruler of the universe and all that is in it. We have no rights; we are His subjects whether we like it or not. Fighting against Him or against His law is foolishness. Besides, as we have noted, He already knows what is best for us anyway. We just need to follow Him and His ways, and all will work for our best in all things.

"But God hath chosen... that no flesh should glory in His presence"(1 Corinthians 1:27-29). Clearly, we have no rights to challenge the choices of God, except to know that whatever He does is the very best for us. He always does good. We cannot brag that we achieved anything or deserve anything from Him but He wishes to do good to us, to give us life and all things good. Our choices are at best incomplete and incompetent but, since He knows what we need before we even ask, He works all things together for our good (Romans 8:28).

God is Personal -- "Who [Jesus] being the brightness of His [God's] glory and the express image of His person" (Hebrews 1:3).

God is a Person, with personality, and deals with humans personally, not remotely, from some great distance somewhere. He is not like the god of deists, who built the universe, like a clock, and set it in motion so that then He lets it and everyone in it run on its own power. God is involved constantly with the running of the universe and with the lives of each human being (Hebrews 1:3; Matthew 10:29-31). He answers personal prayers (Philippians 4:6-7) and implements plans for each human being's life (John 15:16; 1 Corinthians 2:9; Ephesians 1:4-5; 2:10). He knows our every need, our thoughts, our desires (Psalm 37: 18, 23), our concerns, and works to make all things work together for our good (Romans8:28).

God is Good -- "And He [Jesus] said unto him, Why callest thou me good? There is none good but one, that is, God:" (Matthew 19:17).

Good is defined by God. Good is what God is. We know good because He has revealed Himself to us and what good is. Bad is that which is not God. He embodies all that is good in existence. Involved in His goodness are the characteristics of graciousness, mercy, love, and kindness. Grace means undeserved favor. Mercy is treating the guilty as though they were innocent; not punishing those who deserve to be punished.

Lovingkindness is the Hebrew word *hesed*, which means love which works through kindness. Love is not always warm fuzzy nice feelings. Sometimes love requires discipline and correction, the inflicting of pain in order to prevent greater evil or suffering. But since there are no innocent people and we all deserve to go to hell, His blessing of mercy and forgiveness is undeserved, freely given by Him, which we cannot earn or achieve.

"But thou art a God ready to pardon, gracious and merciful, slow to anger, and of great kindness..." (Nehemiah 9:17).

Clearly God is much more patient that we would be. We would like to see some people punished immediately for their nasty attitudes or wicked actions, but God is "ready to pardon." He is always gracious and merciful. He is slow to get angry and desires to bestow good things upon us. But all these things come on His terms, not ours. He will always be the Lord; we will never be in charge of our world. We only need to come to Him and ask (see Matthew 7:7).

"...His greatness is unsearchable... The LORD is gracious and full of compassion, slow to anger, and of great mercy. The LORD is good to all and His tender mercies are over all His works" (Psalm 145:3,5, 8-9, 17).

Grace and mercy are terms that continually appear in Scripture to describe God. It is His nature to bestow favor and forgive our sins. It is also His nature to be good. We only know what good is by comparing our own acts with His nature. We could have been made like all the other animals, not even knowing that good and evil exist, but God made us in His image, to be self-aware and to conceive of the notion of "good." God is good to all His creation, even when we do not appreciate or recognize it. It is His nature to do good. The blasphemous picture of God as an angry, vindictive heavenly policeman, ready to strike us down whenever we make a mistake is so far from the reality. Read this passage again, maybe twenty times until we get the real picture of the only good God.

"The works of the LORD are great, sought out of all them that have pleasure therein. His work is honorable and glorious, and His righteousness endureth forever. He hath made His wonderful works to be remembered; the LORD is gracious and full of compassion..." (Psalm 111:2-9).

There are many reasons why the Lord performed mighty miracles in history and had them recorded in the Bible. One major reason is that we remember them, that they were performed by God through human instruments. Only God can do miracles; so-called miraculous events done by pagans are no more than slight of hand, tricks, illusions, and deceptions. God's miracles show us that He has this great power that no one else has, that He cares for His people enough to do great works on our behalf, and that He is imminent, which means He is here on earth with us. He is not a God who is so far away from us that we cannot relate to Him at all. He is Immanuel, God with us, here, now. His mercy, grace, and kindness towards us should draw us to Him. Certainly if He were cruel and vicious, no one would be interested in having a fear-based relationship with a god like that.

"Oh give thanks unto the LORD for He is good, for His mercy endureth forever..." (Psalm 136:1-9).

His goodness evokes thanksgiving from us. How grateful we should be for all His goodness and kindness. Just think how horrible existence would be if He did not exist or was not good to us. Our human inclination is toward evil (see Genesis 6) and we would living in chaos, destroying each other and everything around us. Though we suffer somewhat now, because of our sin and the evil nature of fallen man, think what it would be like if there were no restraints, no order, no kindness or goodness in anyone.

"Blessed be the God even the Father of our Lord Jesus Christ, the Father of mercies and the God of all comfort" (2 Corinthians 1:3).

Surely the Scriptures testify that God's heart is love and that He desires to save and comfort His people. Nothing can stop Him from loving and helping us; not the devil, not other people, not even ourselves (Romans 8).

These passages are familiar and obvious, describing God for us. But even in passages that seem not to describe God, we can see Him.

"If thou buy a Hebrew slave, six years shall he serve, and in the seventh he shall go out free"(Exodus 21:2).

The entire 21st chapter of Exodus is a set of laws about the way we should treat other people in business, crime, and social relationships. What does this chapter tell us about God Himself? First, He is clearly concerned that we treat people right, with kindness and fairness. So He treats people right as well. He is kind and fair, according to His plans for us. We may not recognize it at first, but He eventually reveals His purposes and how He has worked all things together for our good.

What a wonderful God He is, how much He cares for us, how much He has done to rescue us from ourselves and from the kingdom of darkness! Think about His great goodness and His great power to do good. We should have nothing but love for Him and trust in His good nature and His good ways to live.

"When the Lord thy God shall bring thee into the land whither thou goest to possess it and hath cast out many nations before thee, . . . and when the Lord thy God shall deliver them before thee, thou shalt smite them and utterly destroy them (Deuteronomy 7:1-2).

To many people, God sounds like an ogre in passages like these but, on the contrary, He is trying to save His people from great sin, death, and misery. In Deuteronomy 6:18, God explains "and thou shalt do that which is right and good in the sight of the Lord, that it may be well with you . . ." It was so easy for His people to be tempted by the religions of the Canaanites, which were based on sensuality and resulted in horrible, evil actions like burning their own children to appease their deities, indiscriminate sex with temple prostitutes of both sexes, purposeless loss of life, and much suffering and hopelessness.

God had to show them the better way, the right ways of living that would protect them from such evil. He has shown us today the way of rescue in Christ, the way of freedom from the kingdom of darkness and eternal suffering. The people of Israel had to remove the evil from the land so that they would prosper by living God's way. These Canaanites has been given over four hundred years to respond to His law and they refused (see Genesis 15:13-16). They were not innocent, sweet people. God is infinitely more patient with people than we are. See Ahab's story in 1 Kings 21, especially verse 29. So for Israel's protection and success, those people had to be gone from Palestine. This reveals God's mercy (400 years of patience), protection of His people, and His providence (supply) for His own. He also hates sin and the results of sinful behavior, which is so destructive to His people. Sin also eventually gets punished and removed from God's people.

"And the Lord turned the captivity of Job, when he prayed for his friends; also the Lord gave Job twice as much as he had before" (Job 42:10-12).

The book of Job is not about the suffering innocents. Job does suffer in the book but the Lord never answers any of his or his friends' questions. The book is about the sovereignty of God. He is the one in charge of the world; He is the one under whom all creatures, including Satan and all angels and all people, are subject. He is the King of the universe to whom all must submit. The book shows us that not only is He sovereign but He interacts with His creation, and blesses His people, despite their weaknesses and errors in judgment. Job made all kinds of accusations of God yet he was forgiven and blessed. He admitted "I have uttered that which I understood not." God also makes things work for our good, in spite of Satan's attempts to destroy us, in spite of all our stupidity, and in spite of others' well-meaning but misplaced considerations. We see His sovereignty, omnipotence, kindness, love, and personal attention in this book.

Look for God's nature in the Bible. We will not make mistakes in our theology if we see Him in everything as opposed to judging things by our current cultural values and practices. Continue to practice seeing Him in all the books of the Bible; the more you know what He is like, the more you will understand about life. "Be not conformed to this world but be transformed by the renewing of your mind, that ye may prove what is that good and acceptable and perfect will of God" (Romans 12:2).

CHAPTER TWO
The Work of Christ

Everything that pertains to us is **in Christ**. We are justified in Christ; we are sanctified in Christ; we are glorified in Christ. Our relationship with the Father is in Christ. We are heirs of Christ, children of God in Christ. Our sins were taken away in Christ. Everything we have and everything we are, is in Christ. The whole point of Christianity is Christ. It is not about what we can do for Him; it's about what He's done for us.

Let us be reminded of a major point. Theological concepts are NOT objects or things. Words like salvation, sanctification, justification, glorification, reconciliation, adoption, and so on are NOT objects or things to be possessed or handled. So it is impossible for us to lose an object which we never possessed. Salvation means "rescued," an action and an attitude on the part of God. We are never given salvation; we are instead rescued from slavery to sin and we are given the Holy Spirit, who causes us to live eternally. But we are never given a thing called salvation, so it is impossible to lose "having been rescued."

It is equally impossible to lose "having been set apart by God for His purposes (sanctification)," or to lose "having been considered as if we had never sinned (justification)" in our relationship to God and His law. See what I mean? God did something in Christ beyond atoning for our sins (atonement). From His grace (favor) because He loves us, He rescued us from sin and its inevitable punishment (salvation). He set us apart from all other creatures for His purposes (sanctification) and now considers us who are born-again Christians as if we had never sinned against Him (justification). He has prepared an eternal body and home for us to live with

Him for eternity in a new earth and has placed His glory upon us (glorification). He has reconciled us (brought us back together) to Himself in Christ so that we are no longer enemies and strangers to Him (reconciliation). He has adopted us as children through Christ and, because we are in Christ, we receive all the blessings of the kingdom of God as joint-heirs of the kingdom with Christ (adoption).

See? Everything is in Christ. We are in Christ. There was nothing we could have ever done to have deserved these blessings. We cannot earn any of them. God in Christ did it all. We simply receive them through the gift of the Holy Spirit and the new birth He causes to happen to us. We believe, not as an activity of merit, not as an action that earns anything, but in response to the gospel, the good news that all of this is true and that Christ has done it for us ("Faith cometh by hearing and hearing by the word of God" [Romans 10:17]).

In the gospel of John we see Jesus involved in Creation, in 1:1-3 identified as the Logos, the Greek notion of the Eternal Mind. The first chapter of John sets the stage for a study of the truly spiritual understanding of the mission and message of Christ, not simply an historical account of His actions in time. As John points out in the concluding sections, "...these are written that ye might believe that Jesus is the Christ, the Son of God and that believing ye might have life through His name" (John. 20:31), this particular Gospel is distinctly evangelical.

The first step is to equate Christ with the God of Creation. **"In the beginning was the Logos...and the Logos was God" (John 1:1).** Greek philosophy made it clear that there was some eternal something out there, the source of all thought and reason and ideas, a divine

Mind from which all things derive. Their view however did not allow the Eternal Mind to be a personal God who related directly with individuals. But this Mind was the source of all reason and existence. John says in 1:1 that this Logos, this divine Mind, is the God of the Bible, tying the Greek notions to biblical thought.

The same concept appears in Genesis 1, the Hebrew view that a personal God (Elohim) created everything out of the thoughts of His own mind. Thus all things were made by Him and all things belong to Him; "in God, who created all things by Christ Jesus" (Ephesians 3:9); **" For by Him (Christ) were all things created that are in heaven and that are in earth, visible and invisible, whether they be thrones or dominions or principalities or powers; all things were created by Him and for Him," (Colossians 1:16).**

In His life and ministry on earth, Jesus identified Himself as God, which was the problem that the Pharisees had with Him. They acknowledged His miracles but were ready to pick up stones to kill Him because He identified Himself as Divine. **"Therefore the Jews sought the more to kill Him because He not only had broken the Sabbath but said also that God was His father, making Himself equal with God" (John 5:18); "Let this mind be in you which was also in Christ Jesus who, being in the form of God, thought it not robbery to be equal with God but made Himself of no reputation and took upon Himself the form of a servant and was made in the likeness of men..." (Philippians 2:5-7).**

Even more, Christ made it very clear that He may look like an ordinary man but He was indeed God; "And the Word was made flesh and dwelt among us..." (John 1:14); "I and my Father are One" (John 10:30); "...he that hath seen Me hath seen the Father..." (John 14:9); "...of whom as concerning the flesh Christ came, who is over all, God blessed forever" (Romans 9:5); "Looking for that blessed hope and the glorious appearing of the great God and our Savior Jesus Christ" (Titus 2:13). There are many passages that highlight the designation "Son of God" as the identity of Jesus. "God . . . hath in these last days spoken unto us by His Son, whom He appointed heir of all things, by whom He made the worlds, who being the brightness of His glory and the express image of His person..."(Hebrews1:2-3);   "He gave His only begotten Son ," (John 3:16); and others like Matthew 3:17; 4:3; 11:27; 14:33; 16:16; 17:5; 26:53, 63, 64; Mark 1:1; 3:11; 5:7; 14:61, 62; Luke 1:32-35; 4:41; John 1:34; Romans 1:4; 1 Corinthians 1:9; 2 Corinthians 1:19; 1 John 1:7, 23; 5:5, 20; 2 John 3.

The personal name of God in the Old Testament is Jehovah, indicating His divinity and His saving attitude, typified in the form given to Moses in Exodus 3, "I AM." This name also indicates God's eternal existence and timelessness. Jesus definitely and intentionally uses this designation for Himself in John 8:58 talking to the Jews **"Verily, verily, I say unto you, before Abraham was, I AM,"** which provoked the Jews to pick up stones to stone Him. Before Abraham even existed, Jesus is; before the world existed, Jesus is; before anything existed, Jesus is. Clearly this statement is a description of the everlasting Deity, the God who has always existed. "Now , O Father, glorify thou me with thine own self with the glory I had with thee before the world was" (John 17:5).

The Bible was written in many forms of literature, including figurative language. One of the major elements of figurative language used in John, and other passages, is the metaphor, where a generally unrelated descriptive term or name is applied to someone or something. The metaphor is connected to the subject of the description by some form of the verb "to be." The Lord used these terms for Himself to get us to see the spiritual reality that He has brought us. Indeed, He said, "... the words I have spoken to you are spirit and life" (John 6:63) intending for us to look beyond the merely physical and scientific to "see the kingdom of God." Let's look at some of these metaphors.

Jesus said, **"I am the bread of heaven" (John 6:35**). Obviously He is not literally wheat and yeast so He indicates that He represents real spiritual food, for which we hunger and thirst. He is the only source of real food for the soul, the sustenance that fulfills and strengthens us for eternity. We will receive all the spiritual food necessary from Him. In fact, that is the goal, to feed ourselves on His word and presence, not depend on food from some preacher or teacher (see I Corinthians 3:1-2; Hebrews 5:12-14).

"I am the light of the world" (John 8:12). Jesus brings the light of truth and reality which diffuses all darkness. That's why we should be walking in the light, so we know and experience truth, not deceit and falsehood. It seems that we are so easily deceived nowadays, looking for the image of things rather than the substance. That's why we let church leaders with poor characters lead us, and why we vote for people with image but promote destructive political philosophies and exhibit scandalous lives. So many non-Christian religions proliferate the world for the same reason. We walk in fellowship with Christ when we walk in the light (1 John 1:7) and He shows us the way to live.

"I am the door" (John 10:9). There is no way into the grace of God, into life eternal and everlasting joy, except through Christ. All religions are NOT many ways to God but many ways away from God. Only in Christ is the truth and He is the way in to peace with God, forgiveness of sins, redemption from slavery to sin, and the solution to all human problems. All the other "ways" to God promise bliss but produce agony, fear, and anxiety. He is the only way.

"I am the good shepherd" (John 10:11). To understand this passage well, we must look at the shepherd image of God in the 23rd Psalm. "The LORD is my shepherd, I shall lack nothing." Sheep are not the brightest animals in the farmyard. They appear to be nearsighted and nearly defenseless. One dog can direct a herd and one wolf can decimate a large number of them. Sheep can get "lost" by not recognizing the rest of the herd nearby because of the nearsightedness. Goats, on the hand, are clever but rebellious. Sheep, not rebellious but stupid, need the help of the shepherd so, for us, the Lord is the shepherd, the one who leads us, feeds us, protects us, and heals our wounds. Remember, the rod is for the enemies; the staff is to help pull us out of dangers and difficult places. The shepherd does not beat the sheep. He is patient and caring, covering our stupidities and inadequacies. Goodness and mercy comes upon us always from His grace.

"I am the resurrection and the life" (John 11:25). The greatest enemy, death, is only conquered by Christ's resurrection. No other religion has such a promise. Christ's resurrection demonstrated that He is the Son of God. No other religious founder or leader can say that. The cross took care of the sin problem but the resurrection brought life. He has overcome everything detrimental to us, and in Him is life. **"For as the Father hath life in Himself, so hath He given to the Son to have life in Himself" (John 5:26), and "Ye search the scriptures for in them ye think ye have eternal life**

and they are they which testify of Me and ye will not come to Me that ye might have life"(John 5:39-40). Life is not in religious observances, rituals, speaking scriptures, religious formulas, performing good deeds, or any other actions on our part. Life is in a Person, in Jesus Christ. If we are not in Christ, we do not have eternal life, which is why we must be born again, born of God not of blood, flesh, or man. This is a spiritual rebirth, but one that changes our hearts, our perspectives about reality, our desires, our goals, and our ways of life.

"I am the way, the truth, and the life" (John 14:6). We know the way to God only through Christ. We know what God is like only in Christ ("He that hath seen Me hath seen the Father..." John 14:9). He is the visible image of the invisible God (Colossians 1:15). That image which Christ exhibited was Father, not some transcendent Deity completely separated from all His creatures, but Father who loves and cares for each person. The Jews of the times of the New Testament thought themselves distant from God, essentially alone in the world to fight out a meager existence. But Jesus spent a large amount of time trying to get people to see God as Father, involved in every human's life, counting all the hairs on our heads, alert to every sparrow that falls, and so loved the world that He provided the solution to our troubles (John 3:16).

"I am the true vine" (John 15:1). Jesus is the source of all we need. He said we are but branches of the Vine, offshoots of Himself, sent to bless the world. Without Him, we can do nothing of any good (John 15:5). We are not the strong ones; He is the power. We do not receive tools from Him; we are the tools He uses with His power. We draw all our strength from Him. He supplies all we need. He knows we cannot defeat the world "but be of good cheer, I have overcome the world" (John

16:33). In Him we are more than conquerors (Romans 8:37).

Notice other identifying aspects of Christ in the New Testament such as in Him we are already sanctified, redeemed, righteous, and have wisdom available to us. **"He . . . is made unto us wisdom, and righteousness and sanctification, and redemption" (1 Corinthians 1:30).** We are also justified in Him, cleansed from all the stain of sin. **"But ye are washed but ye are sanctified but ye are justified in the name of the Lord Jesus Christ and by the Spirit of our God (1 Corinthians 6:11).** And we, the called of God, are preserved, protected, kept by Him. **" ... to them that are sanctified by God the Father and preserved in Jesus Christ and called," (Jude 1).**

In Christ, we have everything we need and He has given us "every spiritual blessing" **(Ephesians. 1:3).** Notice He is our peace with God and with other people, **"For He is our peace" (Ephesians 2:14).** He started us in our faith and He will complete our journey. **"Jesus the author and finisher of our faith, ...the mediator of the new covenant" (Hebrews 12:2, 24).** We need no other Lord and Master; we need no other Source, for personal Christian living and ministry. **"Christ is all and in all" (Colossians 3:11); "I am the Alpha and Omega" (Revelation 22:13). "He is head of the church" (Ephesians 5:23).**

Properly, we must rid ourselves of thinking that the Church is ours. Thinking that way means that we really think the Church is basically another human social organization. Wrong! We are the Church and Christ is the head of all churches, which means we should find out what He wants to do with us and do that. Let's avoid our own little personal agendas since He won't let them succeed in the church anyway. We won't know what to do or how to do it without Him. If we try, our little church indeed becomes a fruitless, useless social club. What is really important anyway? Only His agenda, His plan will always bring fruit.

"[He is the] great high priest" (Hebrews 4:14). A priest's role has always been to help connect the people with God. In our finite limited knowledge and awareness, we often fail to discern the person and will of God. Jesus, the great High Priest, brought us to the Father through His own blood and resurrection. Through Him, we experience relationship with the Creator of the universe, creatures connected to our Lord and Master in a loving way. When we relinquish full control of our lives to Him, things will always be better. It is useless and vain to fight against Him, to assert our own way, to insist that we know best about ourselves. What could be more ridiculous!

"...in Him dwells the fullness of the Godhead bodily" (Colossians 2:9). Fullness means all there is; there is no weakness or lack in Christ and, as we are in Him, we can experience the same life of fullness.

What Has Jesus Done?

Salvation

Most Christians think of Jesus in connection to the doctrine of salvation, probably because of the most familiar New Testament passage, **"For God so loved the world that He gave His only begotten Son that whosoever believeth in Him should not perish but have everlasting life" (John 3:16).** Indeed, that is a major aspect of the life of Jesus, to seek and to save that which was lost. He has rescued (saved) us from sin and death, as we will see in these passages:

" [He is] come to save [rescue] that which was lost;" (Matthew 18:11).

". . . that you might have life [in Christ]"(John 5:1-40).

"He shall save [rescue] His people from their sins" (Matthew 1:21).

"Neither is there salvation [rescue] in any other . . ." (Acts 4:12).

"We believe that through the grace of our Lord Jesus Christ we shall be saved [rescued]"; (Acts 15:11).

"He might [will] deliver [rescue] us from this present evil world"; (Galatians 1:4).

"For unto you is born today in the city of David a Savior [Rescuer], which is Christ the Lord;" (Luke 2:11).

"For God so loved the world that He gave His only begotten Son, that whosoever believeth in Him should not perish but have everlasting life; for God sent not His Son into the world to condemn the world but that the world through Him might be saved;" (John 3:16-17).

"And said unto the woman, Now we believe, not because of thy saying; for we have heard Him ourselves and know that this is indeed the Christ, the Savior [Rescuer] of the world;" (John 4:42).

"...but these things I say that ye might be saved [rescued];" (John 5:34).

"My sheep hear my voice and I know them and they follow me; and I give them eternal life and they shall never perish, neither shall any one pluck them from out of my hand;" (John 10:27-28).

"I am come a light into the world that whosoever believeth on me should not abide in darkness. And if any man hear my words and believeth not, I judge him not for I came not to judge the world but to save [rescue] the world;" (John 12:46-47).

"Him [Jesus] hath God exalted with His right hand to be a Prince and a Savior [Rescuer]..." (Acts 5:31).

"Of this man's seed [David] hath God according to His promise, raised unto Israel a Savior [Rescuer], Jesus;" (Acts 13:23).

"And they said, Believe on the Lord Jesus Christ, and thou shalt be saved [rescued], and thy house;" (Acts 16:31).

"Therefore by the deeds of the law there shall no flesh be justified in His sight; for by the law is the knowledge of sin. But now the righteousness of God without the law is manifested, being witnessed by the law and the prophets, even the righteousness of God which is by faith of Jesus Christ unto all and upon all them that believe;" (Romans 3:20-22).

"For if, when we were enemies, we were reconciled to God by the death of His Son, much more being reconciled we shall be saved [rescued] by His life;" (Romans 5:10).

"That if thou shalt confess with thy mouth the Lord Jesus and shalt believe in thine heart that God hath raised Him from the dead, thou shalt be saved [rescued];" (Romans 10:9).

"For the preaching of the Cross is to them that perish foolishness, but unto us which are saved [rescued] it is the power of God;" (1 Corinthians 1:18).

"Who hath saved [rescued] us and called us with a holy calling not according to our works but according to His own purpose and grace which was given us in Christ Jesus before the world began but is now made manifest by the appearing of our Savior [Rescuer] Jesus Christ;" (2 Timothy 1:9-10).

"Therefore I endure all things for the elect's sakes, that they may also obtain the salvation [rescue] which is in Christ Jesus with eternal glory;" (2 Timothy 2:10).

"And being made perfect [complete], he [Jesus] became the author of eternal salvation [rescue] unto all them that obey Him" (Hebrews 5:9).

Do we really need more passages? These are just a few of many more verses of Scripture that show us what salvation means. Clearly, the way for us to be rescued from the slavery to sin is in Christ. He is the Savior, the Rescuer. That's why our salvation, our rescue, is effected by Him, since it is His action and attitude to rescue us, not some entity, some object, we earn by doing good works.

Life

Jesus has given us Life, not improved our earthly lives. He has made us live. Life is in a Person, not in religious observances, rituals, prayers, reading scriptures, or anything else. Jesus told the Pharisees, **"Ye**

search the scriptures, for in them ye think ye have eternal life, and they are they which testify of me. And ye will not come to me that ye might have life" (John 5:39-40). Just reading Scriptures will not bring us life. Life is only in Him, in a Person, Jesus. The Pharisees knew Scriptures but had no life and would not come to the giver of life.

He further said to them that **"I am come that they [His sheep] might have life, and that they might have it more abundantly" (John 10:10).** Notice the definition of abundant life in John 10. The thief came to kill, steal, and destroy. Jesus came to give us just the opposite of that. He came to give us life, to provide for all our needs, and to build us up. That is the true definition of abundant life. No fear of destruction, sufficient supply for us to live on earth, and encouragement, trust, and confidence (true faith) in Him. Abundance does not necessarily mean riches, fame, and fortune. Those are American cultural values, not biblical promises. But we should expect *shalom*, which means that everything is well with us (see Philippians 4:19).

Paul's writings add to this truth, **"Christ who hath abolished death and has brought life" (2 Timothy 1:10). "I am crucified with Christ, yet I live but not I but Christ liveth in me (Galatians 2:20).** Not only has Jesus brought life, He lives in us. That means He is with us always, not outside us somewhere far away. He is living though us so that people in the world see Him in us. We have been given the life eternal (Romans 6:23) and we shine in a dark world because He shines through us.

"Therefore if any man be in Christ, he is a new creature, old things are passed away"

(2 Corinthians 5:17). We are new creatures in Christ. He is in us and we are in Him. There is a union in our relationship, hence we have received all the necessary and desirable blessings because we are in Him. Everything we are and everything we have is in Him. Therefore we are new beings, new creations, regenerated with life eternal, persons in a relationship of life and love with the Creator through Christ. And He is in us, not off somewhere away from us. We don't need to be asking Him to come to us; He is already in us.

"You He made alive who were dead. . . (Ephesians 2:1). "Even when we were dead in sins hath [He] made us alive together with Christ," (Ephesians 2:5). "The wages of sin is death but the gift of God is eternal life through Jesus Christ our Lord" (Romans 6:23). The gift of Life is just that, a gift; nothing we can earn or deserve, for we are all saved by God's grace [unmerited favor], according to His good pleasure and purpose, not according to our righteousness (Ephesians 2:8-9; Ephesians 1:3-6). This life is eternal, which means we have been made able to live in His presence forever.

Justification

Jesus has removed our sins, taken them on Himself, and sent them away from us forever. **"The Lamb of God which taketh away the sin of the world," (John 1:29; see John 6:51). "He... purged our sins," (Hebrews 1:3). "Christ died for our sins," (1 Corinthians 15:3).** We are now, in Christ, justified before God, just as if we had never sinned at all. We do not have a past life now, but a blessed future life. He has separated us from our sins as far as the east is from the west, which means an impossible distance. The guilt of our sins is gone for good. The main reason for all His effort is that He loves us. **"Unto Him that loved us and washed us from our sins in His own blood . . ."** (Revelation 1:5).

He destroyed the work of the devil.

The work of the devil is, and has always been, to deceive humans and try to inspire us to disobey God's will. He began by deceiving some of the angelic host, then Eve in the Garden, and then Cain and the rest of humanity, except for Noah. Notice he cannot literally physically touch or attack humans or we all would have been killed by him. The devil's greatest weapon is fear. Jesus' sacrifice and resurrection put an end to the need for us to fear anything from the devil; **"the purpose of the Son of God...destroy the works of the devil;"** (1 John 3:8). **"[He] has delivered us from the power of darkness;"** (Colossians 1:12-13).

He loves us.

No one need be without love; God loves everyone, whether we all recognize it or not. **"God so loved the world that He gave His only begotten Son, that whosoever believeth in Him should not perish but have eternal life"** (John 3:16). His desire is that we recognize His sacrifice, suffering greatly on our behalf, and become new creations, born again by His Spirit, so that He and we have a voluntary relationship. He did not want creatures who related to Him like robots, without a desire like His to love each other.

"Herein is love, not that we loved God, but that He loved us, and sent His Son to be the propitiation for our sins" (1 John 4:10). **"He is the propitiation for our sins,"** (1 John 2:2). He paid the punishment for our transgressions. Propitiate means "to appease or satisfy the anger of" and "to gain the favor of." So by His death on the Cross, Jesus satisfied the necessity to punish sin and gained for us the favor of God. Otherwise, we would still be the objects of God's wrath and without His favor. Jesus achieved a monumental blessing for us, which we can never fully appreciate nor comprehend.

He has sanctified us.
"... that the offering of the Gentiles might be acceptable, sanctified by the Holy Spirit" (Romans 15:16). "And such were some of you. But you were washed; but you were sanctified; but you were justified in the name of the Lord Jesus and by the Spirit of our God" (1 Corinthians 6:11). "... because God from the beginning chose you for salvation through sanctification by the Spirit and belief in the truth ..." (2 Thessalonians 2:13).

So many Christians have believed that, after Christ has saved us, we must work very hard to become "sanctified" or essentially sinless, or at least mostly sinless. Otherwise we have failed to become "good" Christians and end up fruitless and barely able to enter heaven at the end. What rubbish! What deception and bondage! From just the passages above, we should be able to see clearly enough that we have already been "sanctified" in Christ. "Sanctify" means to set apart from one use to another. We have been set apart from other humans to God as His beloved children.

As Galatians 3 teaches us, we came to Christ by faith; He expects us to live by faith as well, trusting in the working of the Holy Spirit, not in the capabilities of our own strength. Spiritual discipline is good, so Paul says, but we are not going to make ourselves righteous; Jesus has already done that. We are not going to make ourselves holy; He has already done that. We are not going to make ourselves powerful; He has already done that too. Get away from teaching that stresses all the things you have to do to get God to help you or bless you or empower you. Been there, done that!!

He has become all things for us.

Notice all that Jesus has done for us and has become for us, so that, in Him, we have everything. " **He is our sanctification;" (1 Corinthians 6:11; Jude 1; Hebrews 10:10).** He prepared an eternal place for us to be with Him, so that we look forward to eternal life with Him. There is no such thing as annihilation or non-existence for us. We will not be just assumed into the divine energy, or become just another element in a self-perpetuating everlasting universe. We will always be persons, in relationship with Christ always. **"Let not your hearts be troubled, ye believe in God, believe also in me. In my Father's house are many dwelling places; if it were not so, I would have told you. I go to prepare a place for you, and if I go and prepare a place for you, I will come again and receive you unto myself, that where I am, there ye may be also" (John 14:1-3).**

He has given us peace; there is NO condemnation for us who are in Him. **"In me you may have peace;" (John 16:33). "Therefore, having been justified by faith, we have peace with God;" (Romans 5:1-2). "There is therefore now no condemnation to them which are in Christ..." (Romans 8:1).** He has given us freedom in Christ and everything necessary to live righteously; **"According as His divine power hath given unto us all things that pertain unto life and godliness, through the knowledge of Him that hath called us to glory and virtue;" (2 Peter 1:3).**

So since we have been given so much including the capability to live righteously, to be lights to the world, and to receive the blessings of God, then we should do so.

Just do it. It's all there, in you already. You don't have to try hard to make it happen. You don't have to perform rituals or formulas to receive anything from God. He has already given it; He already hears your prayers; He already has empowered His church through the Holy Spirit who lives in us now. We keep trying to live like Old Testament people, thinking God is beyond us somewhere and we must do things just right to get Him to bless and help us. No, that won't work. He is in us and with us. We can't get closer to Him. We can become more aware of His presence but He is right here, ready to help us and relate to us and allow us to minister with Him. Go do it!

CHAPTER THREE
The Ministry of the Holy Spirit

First, let's understand some basic principles that will guide our understanding of the nature and work of the Holy Spirit. To begin with, the Holy Spirit is God. **"But when the Comforter is come, whom I will send unto you from the Father, even the Spirit of truth which proceedeth from the Father, he shall testify of Me" (John 15:26).** The Holy Spirit proceeds from the Father; God from God; He is Trinity-defined.

In the Book of Acts, ... **"the Holy Spirit said, 'Separate [to] Me Barnabas and Saul for the work where unto I have called them ... So they, being sent forth by the Holy Spirit, departed unto Seleucia ..." (Acts 13:1-4).**
The Holy Spirit called them and sent them out to ministry. The Holy Spirit forbade Paul and Barnabas to preach in Asia (Acts 16:6-10) and "moved" the prophets to write the Scriptures (2 Peter 1:20-21). Clearly the Holy Spirit talks and acts like we hear God talking and acting in other passages of Scripture and He certainly possesses all the prerogatives and characteristics of deity.

He is a Person, not a magic fluid, or cosmic energy, or spiritual "fuel" that can be obtained or imparted as an object to be possessed by human beings. He possesses us. He, the Person of the Holy Spirit, dwells in us and never leaves us. **"Know ye not that ye are the temple of God and that the Spirit of God dwelleth in you?" (1 Corinthians 3:16-17). "That good thing which was committed unto thee, keep by the Holy Spirit which dwelleth in us" (2 Timothy 1:14).**

The Holy Spirit, as a Person, does not leave us, nor "leak out" or burn up within us, such that we periodically need a re-fill, a "fresh" infilling or anointing. When we were saved and born again, we were indwelt by Him, all of Him, forever. We have received all the Holy Spirit we will ever have; we have received all the power we will ever have since He is the power. He is the power; we don't possess some spiritually autonomous power to use on our own. We know from experience as well, that our "use" of spiritual power is limited and incomplete. Not everyone we pray for gets healed; not every miracle we ask for or try to accomplish happens. Not everyone we say a prayer over gets saved. The reason is that He is the one who accomplishes, saves, heals. Not us. It's not our power or righteousness that saves or heals; it's His. We do not receive tools; WE are the tools, in the hands of the Master Workman. We need to get out of our minds that we are anything but channels of His will and power. Jesus said, **"Without Me, ye can do nothing"** (John **15:5).**

Notice these Scriptures:

> **"Repent and be baptized every one of you in the name of Jesus Christ for the remission of sins and *ye shall receive the gift of the Holy Spirit*"** (Acts 2:38).

> **"And we are His witnesses to these things, and so also is *the Holy Spirit whom God hath given* to them that obey Him"** (Acts 5:32).

> **"... who, when they were come down, prayed for them that they might *receive the Holy Spirit*, for as yet He was fallen upon none of them. Only they were baptized in the name of the Lord Jesus. Then laid they their hands on them and they received the Holy Spirit. And when Simon saw that through laying on of the apostles' hands *the Holy Spirit was given*, he offered them money saying, Give me also this power. ...But Peter said unto him, 'Thy money perish with thee because thou hast thought that the gift of God may be purchased with money!'"** (Acts 8:12-19).

"While Peter thought on the vision, the Spirit said to him, ... While Peter yet spake these words, the Holy Spirit fell on all them which heard the word; and they of the circumcision which believed were astonished, because *that on the Gentiles also was poured out the gift of the Holy Spirit*" (Acts 10:19, 38, 45-48).

"And as I began to speak, the Holy Spirit fell on them as on us at the beginning. For as much then as *God gave them the same gift as He did unto us* who believed on the Lord Jesus Christ, what was I that I could withstand God?" (Acts 11:15-17).

"And hope maketh not ashamed because the love of God is shed abroad in our hearts by *the Holy Spirit which is given unto us*" (Romans 5:5).

"Now *we have received*, not the spirit of the world, but *the Spirit which is of God* that we might know the things that are freely given to us of God; which things also we speak not in the words which man's wisdom teacheth but which the Holy Spirit teacheth, comparing spiritual things with spiritual" (1 Corinthians 2:10-15).

The Holy Spirit **IS** the Gift that we have received at conversion, not some spiritual force or substance or endowments of abilities. HE is the power; HE is the One who gets the job done. A gift is not earned, by works or by strenuous efforts to believe or pray. A gift is received, with thanksgiving. Through Him, because God favors us, we also received eternal life (Romans 6:23). We don't earn eternal life either; not by works, or being "good" or by getting our lives right or any other action on our part. That is grace. We simply believe the gospel, which we will explain in other parts of this book. We receive the Holy Spirit as a gift and then He comes to dwell in us, individually and collectively as the Church, the Body of Christ. Then He, the Holy Spirit, uses us for His purposes and for the benefit of the Body of Christ (1 Corinthians 12:7, 11).

Perhaps now would be a good time to simply discuss some of the other biblical passages that relate to the Holy Spirit.

"I indeed baptize you with water unto repentance, but He that cometh after me is mightier than I … He shall baptize you with the Holy Spirit and with fire" (Matthew 3:11-12).

John the Baptist in this passage refers to Jesus as the One who comes to baptize in the Holy Spirit. The Greek word "baptize" means to "pour over, to cover completely, to dip into" so Jesus is the One who covers us, or dips us into, the Holy Spirit. We often hear in Scripture that the Holy Spirit is "poured out upon" us, such as in Joel 2 and Acts 2:17-18.

This event is not a continual thing but a once-done happening. In New Testament theology, when the Spirit is poured out on a person, He stays with that person forever (John 14:16-17). There is absolutely no need for a Christian to pray that the Holy Spirit be poured out again or that we need an additional pouring out of the Spirit. That's been done and is permanent. The same is true of the concept of "anointing." The Anointed One, Jesus, lives in us and that's all the "anointing" we are going to get. He is all we need and He is the Anointed One.

To understand the concept of anointing, change the spelling to "Appointed One." Anointing is not power, or spiritual "stuff" that empowers us. The Holy Spirit IS the power, through which Christ operates in us. There is no such "spiritual power," as some kind of substance that we receive to make our ministries more powerful. Power is the most sought-for thing that post-modern people want, but Christians have all the power in heaven and earth living in us, Jesus Christ Himself. What more power could one want?

What more power could one receive? Don't get caught up in the Old Testament concept that one must keeping asking God to give us power. He has already given us everything we need to live a godly, powerful life—the Holy Spirit.

"But as many as received Him, to them gave He power to become the sons of God, even to them that believe on His name, which were born, not of blood, nor of the will of the flesh, nor of the will of man, but of God" (John 1:12-13, 32-34).

First, notice that it is God who gives the authority and power; we do not have it on our own. So we become children of God, not because we did anything special, but that He saves us because of His grace. Grace means "unmerited favor," which means that we do not deserve any favor. We are rebellious, mean-spirited, disobedient creations of God who all deserve to go to hell. There are no innocent people; all have sinned and come short of the glory of God (Romans 3:23). So it is only by the favor of God, by His gift to us of eternal life (Romans 6:23), that we do not deserve, only because of His love, that we are rescued from ourselves and from the kingdom of darkness in which we have lived all our lives. And also notice that we are children, not of flesh (blood) nor of the will of human beings, though it appears that way for physical birth, nor the will of a husband (Greek *andros*), but we are born of God, new creations, given birth by Him, not by anything we do.

"And John bare record saying, 'I saw the Spirit descending from heaven like a dove and it abode on Him ... which baptizeth with the Holy Spirit'" (John 1:32-33).

It wasn't a bird that descended. The verse says "like a dove," which is a simile. We use the picture often, such as "He roared like a lion," or "She sang like an angel." He is clearly NOT a lion but sounded "like" one; she was NOT an angel but sang "like" one. So, "like" a dove descends to earth after flight, so the Holy Spirit resembled a similar descent, coming upon the earthly Christ. The picture of "descending" is like the picture of "pouring out upon," which was used many times previously in the Bible. The Spirit is NOT a bird which must descend after flight, nor spiritual oil to be poured, but these are pictures to which we can relate. The Holy Spirit is a Person, God resident in us.

"... for John truly baptized with water but ye shall be baptized with the Holy Spirit not many days hence ... But ye shall receive power when the Holy Spirit is come upon you and ye shall be witnesses unto Me ..." (Acts 1:4-8).

Again, He is the power which was given to us, which we received. There is power in us because the Power, the Spirit, is in us and with us. The power is NOT us, but Him in us. The obvious point of having the Spirit resident in power in us is for us to be witnesses of Christ to the world.

"... and they were all filled with the Holy Spirit and began to speak with other languages as the Spirit gave them utterance" (Acts 2:1-4).

The word "filled" is an aorist verb tense (see discussion below) and indicates that the filling was incidental (one time action) and the disciples responded to the filling by action. This time, speaking in languages other than their usual Aramaic, the Holy Spirit inspired them and had them speak in a multitude of dialects (local versions of foreign languages) that they would have not known. They did NOT do this on their own or because they perceived that it would be a good thing. All manifestations of the Spirit must come from Him, not our mental or emotional decisions. Too many people "speak in tongues" or prophesy all on their own, without incontrovertible knowledge that the Spirit has led them. We had best be very sure that whatever messages we think we are inspired to speak have in reality come from God, and not our imaginations.

"... and they were all filled with the Holy Spirit and they spoke the word of God with boldness" (Acts 4:31).

Again, in an incidental, one-time, repeatable event, the disciples are "filled" and then spoke. Filling is not for convenience or experience, but for action. We are filled so we can do something in response. The power of the Holy Spirit is manifested for action benefitting the Body of Christ, not just so we can demonstrate that we are "spiritual" or can exercise some mysterious spiritual abilities.

"But the manifestation of the Spirit is given to every man for the profit of all ... But all these worketh that one and the selfsame Spirit, dividing to every man individually as He will" (1 Corinthians 12:7-11).

"Wherefore brethren, look ye out among you seven men of honest report, full of the Holy Spirit and wisdom, ... and they chose Stephen, a man full of faith and the Holy Spirit, ... and Stephen, full of faith and power, did great wonders and miracles, ..." (Acts 6:3-5, 8).

In New Testament Greek, there are several verb tenses which include two vitally important ones as they relate to the phrase "filled with the Holy Spirit:" the imperfect tense and the aorist tense. The tenses usually tend to indicate completed action or past actions, but the imperfect tense is a linear continual action, such as "Paul was preaching to the Athenians." The aorist tense is punctiliar, completed action, a one-time action which could be repeated at times such as "Paul preached to the Athenians today." In every case in the New Testament where the phrase "filled with the Holy Spirit" is used, the aorist tense is employed, NOT the imperfect. Thus the fillings are incidental, one-time events, such as in the passages above Acts 2:1-4 and Acts 4:31. Consider the way it all works.

In the Old Testament, when the Holy Spirit had yet to dwell permanently within believers, all filling of the Holy Spirit was an "outside-in" operation. The Spirit "came upon" people from outside of them. In the New Testament, the Holy Spirit dwells within people, so He does not "come upon" in the literal sense. He is already inside, so filling is an "inside-out" operation, such as in John 7:38-39 where Jesus speaks of the Spirit as rivers of living waters that come from within and "spill out" as it were from inside a believer. So for New Testament believers, the Spirit bursts forth from inside to "fill" us for a specific event or incident, such as prophecy or some miraculous action. In 1 Corinthians 12, we are NOT given "supernatural gifts" to use as we desire, but "the manifestation of the Spirit" (v. 7) is given to each one for the benefit of the body of Christ. We do not possess supernatural abilities; we are slaves of Christ through the Holy Spirit. We don't have tools; we are the tools, used by the Spirit as He wills (v. 11).

In the Acts 6:3-8 passage, the term "full" is equivalent in meaning to a way of saying that someone or something demonstrates a certain character, such as "Thomas is full of joy" which means he is joyful fellow or "Sue is full of wisdom" that means she is a wise woman. It does NOT mean that a substance called "wisdom" literally comes from somewhere and fills her being with itself. We cannot think in scientific, mathematical literality in these passages and hope to understand the message.

"Jesus answered, 'Verily, verily, I say unto thee, except a man be born of water and of the Spirit, he cannot enter into the kingdom of God'" (John 3:5).
This passage indicates that the New Birth is an essential event in the lives of believers. To enter the kingdom

of God, people who are born of water (physical human birth) must also be born of spirit (God). Humans cannot enter the kingdom of God by being good or doing good things in their own natural humanness but must "put on" the new person, given birth by God, so that we may be made able to be in His presence.

"These things I have spoken unto you being yet present with you, but the Comforter which is the Holy Spirit, whom the Father will send in my name, He shall teach you all things, and bring all things to your remembrance whatsoever I have said to you." (John 14:25-26).

We recognize in this passage that the Holy Spirit is called "the Comforter," which literally means "the One called alongside to help." We need help to live rightly; we need help to be witnesses; we need help to overcome the strategies of the devil. So the Holy Spirit is that Comforter, who manifests Himself to bless the Body of Christ with wisdom, knowledge, healing, faith, miracles, and so on. He is that Helper who enables us to live righteously and be effective witnesses to the world. He fulfills the role that Jesus played on earth, walking alongside His disciples. So the Spirit walks alongside us everywhere, all the time. He will teach us, through the Word itself, through teachers of the Word, preaching, experience, mature brothers and sisters in Christ, and by direct speaking to us, all things we need to know and bring to our remembrance what we've learned and been told. Do you need to know something vital? The Holy Spirit will tell you when you need to know. Not to worry.

"... if I go not away, the Comforter will not come unto you, but if I depart, I will send Him unto you, and when He is come, He will reprove the world of sin, and of righteousness and of judgment ... Howbeit when He, the Spirit of truth, is come, He will guide you into all truth,

for He shall not speak of Himself but whatsoever He shall hear that shall he speak and He will show you things to come. He shall glorify Me, for He shall receive of Mine and shall show it unto you" (John 16:7-15).

Besides being "alongside" us, the Holy Spirit convicts the world of its evil rebellion. We must realize that we do not persuade people or convict people of their sins; we preach the Word and the Holy Spirit does the convicting. So, if only one person comes to the altar after you preach the gospel, you have not failed. You cannot convict or save them anyway. That's His business; ours is to proclaim the gospel. John 16 also indicates that the Spirit will tell us of things to come. Prophecy is His message to give, not ours to give of ourselves. We see wrong (in our eyes) and proceed to rebuke it by saying "thus says the Lord," when He hasn't said it at all. We just think He should have. As I have said earlier, be very careful and sure that any message you give is His and not yours. **"And my speech and my preaching were not with enticing words of man's wisdom but in demonstration of the Spirit and of power that your faith should not stand in the wisdom of men but in the power of God" (1 Corinthians 2:4-5).**

There are many passages in Scripture that indicate the personal direction and sovereignty of God the Holy Spirit.
"... they were forbidden by the Holy Spirit to preach the Word in Asia, ... they tried to go into Bithynia but the Spirit did not permit them" (Acts 16:6-10).
"... Paul was compelled by the Spirit ..." (Acts 18:5).
"... except the Holy Spirit witnesseth in every city ... over which the Holy Spirit hath made you overseers, to feed the church of God which He hath purchased with His own blood ... Thus saith the Holy Spirit, so shall the Jews at Jerusalem bind the man that owneth this belt ..." (Acts 20:23, 28; Acts 21:11).

It is abundantly clear that the Holy Spirit is God in the Church, in the Christians, guiding and directing the process of missions and evangelism of the early Church. We must also assume that He has continued to perform that duty throughout the ages so that, even though individual Christians in our imperfection may make mistakes, abuse our positions, even sin dramatically at times, the Holy Spirit never leaves us and continues to work with us so that the Church will be here, ready and willing, when Jesus returns.

CHAPTER FOUR
The Christian Life

Since Christ has done it all, saved us, freed us from sin and the kingdom of darkness, sanctified us, glorified us, and made us complete in Him, what then do we do? We can't make ourselves holier or sinless. And certainly not by disciplining ourselves or by asceticism, fasting, self-suffering, and so on, can we become "better" Christians. We can't gain more power from God than what we already have. We have been given the gift of the Holy Spirit. He is the power, all the power. We have been given everything necessary for life and godliness (2 Peter:1:3-4) and have been blessed with every spiritual blessing in Christ (Ephesians 1:3). Christ has already defeated Satan and all the hosts of wickedness (Colossians 2:13-15). So, do we just sit back and do nothing? No, there are things for us to do.

The apostle James summarized the whole thing in chapter one of his letter. **"Pure religion and undefiled before God and the Father is this: to visit the fatherless and widows in their affliction, and to keep himself unspotted from the world" (James 1:27).** Essentially we minister to others and keep ourselves unstained from worldliness, which is a witness to the world. The issues then are how we do these two things, in the midst of a personal relationship with our Savior.

What follows are samples of Scripture that focus on the many things Christians should do to minister to others and keep ourselves unstained from the world. There are also explanations of the meanings of these passages as they pertain to our instruction in righteousness and walking with God. There are many more but these are the most notable and familiar to most of us.

"Hear, O Israel: The LORD our God is one! Thou shalt love the LORD thy God with all thine heart, with all thy soul, and with all thy might" (Deuteronomy 6:4-5). This phrase simply means that we should love God with our whole selves, with all of ourselves. To love Him means that we should keep his commandments. **"For this is the love of God, that we keep His commandments. And His commandments are not grievous [burdensome]" (1 John 5:3).**

We have been given new natures; we are new creations. The desires of our hearts should be to do things the way Christ wants them done, to love His ways, to want to please Him out of gratitude rather than obligation. So we know His commandments are the best way to live. Remember, He always does what is best for us; He makes all things work together for our good; He always does good. Why would any of us think we know better than He does? So whatever He says we should do, is the best thing to do. If He says forgive those who trespass against us, then regardless of the cruelty we suffer from others, we must treat them as if they hadn't done it. If He says we should pray a certain way, then we should want to do so. He will not tell us to do something that is bad for us.

Many people claim to know Christ but if we do not love Him and His ways and His commandments, we do not know Him. **"Hereby we do know that we know Him, if we keep His commandments. He that saith, 'I know Him,' and keepth not His commandments, is a liar, and the truth is not in him. But whoso keepeth His word, in him verily is the love of God perfected. Hereby know we that we are in Him. He that saith he abideth in Him ought himself also so to walk even as He walked" (1 John 2:3-6).**

"And this is His commandment: that we should believe on the name of His Son Jesus Christ and love one another, as He gave us commandment" (1 John 3:23).

Loving one another is not necessarily having warm fuzzy feelings, as we have mentioned earlier. Love is the determined and intentional action on our parts to do good to others, to care about them and the things that happen to them, to come to their aid in time of difficulty (see I Corinthians 13 for a description of love).

The apostle Paul describes in more practical terms just how we love others in a Christian way in Romans

" For I say, through the grace given unto me, to every man that is among you, not to think of himself more highly than he ought to think, but to think soberly, according as God hath dealt to every man a measure of faith. For as we have many members in one body, and all members have not the same office, so we, being many, are one body in Christ, and every one members one of another.

Having then gifts differing according to the grace that is given to us, if prophecy, let us prophesy according to the proportion of faith; or ministry, let us wait on our ministering; or he that teacheth, on teaching; or he that exhorteth, on exhortation; he that giveth, with simplicity; he that ruleth, with diligence; he that showeth mercy, with cheerfulness.

Let love be without dissimulation [hypocrisy]. Abhor that which is evil. Cleave to that which is good. Be kindly affectioned to one another with brotherly love, in honor preferring one another; not slothful in business, fervent in spirit, serving the Lord; rejoicing in hope, patient in tribulation, continuing instant in prayer; distributing to the necessity of saints, given to hospitality. Bless them which persecute you; bless and curse not. Rejoice with them that do rejoice, and weep with them that weep. Be of the same mind one toward another. Mind not high things, but condescend to men of low estate. Be not wise in your own conceits. Recompense no man evil for evil. Provide things honest in the sight of all men. If it be possible, as much as lieth in you, live peaceably with all men.

Dearly beloved, avenge not yourselves, but rather give place unto wrath; for it is written, 'Vengeance is Mine, I will repay,' saith the Lord. Therefore, if thine enemy hunger, feed him; If he thirst, give him drink; For in so doing thou shalt heap coals of fire on his head. Be not overcome of evil, but overcome evil with good" (Romans 12:3-21).

All of these admonitions simply instruct us in the ways of love, like Jesus did. So we have distinctly specific ways to minister to people, to treat others, in love as James has indicated in James 1:27.

Paul continues in Romans 13 with instruction about the ways of loving others. **"Owe no man anything but to love one another, for he that loveth another hath fulfilled the law. For this, 'Thou shalt not commit adultery, Thou shalt not murder, Thou shalt not steal, Thou shalt not bear false witness, Thou shalt not covet,' and if there be any other commandment, it is briefly comprehended in this saying, namely, 'Thou shalt love thy neighbor as thyself.' Love worketh no ill to his neighbor; therefore love is the fulfilling of the law"** (Romans 13:8-10).

Paul connects God's Ten Commandments with our New Testament ethic; we have been given the capability, as new creations filled with the Holy Spirit, to live in this way of love and freedom. The principles of God's law in the Old Testament, fulfilled in Christ, now become manifested in us who are in Christ and are the Body of Christ. We love the laws and ways of God. He hasn't changed the principles of the ways He's told us to live. Exodus 21 describes the way the people of God should treat Hebrew slaves. Well, we do not have Hebrew slaves, so do we just throw out that section of Scripture? No, we look for the principle, which is that we should treat people under our authority with kindness, dignity, and love. So we look in the Old Testament for the revealing of the nature of God and for principles of right living, supported by New Testament teachings.

Paul's next teaching reveals to us that we have been freed from the domination of sin by the life of Christ. The cross satisfied the Law's requirements and brought us forgiveness of sins. God looks at us just as if we had never sinned at all because Christ took all our sins upon Himself and carried them away. Then, the resurrection defeated death and brought us life; His life is in us and we live in Him.

"There is therefore now no condemnation to them which are in Christ Jesus"(Romans 8:1-11; 28-29). Notice that there is now NO condemnation for us. God has removed the condemnation that our sin had brought but now there is NO more condemnation from Him and should be none from us. Do not condemn yourself. John said that if we confess our sins He is faithful and just to forgive us our sins and cleanse us from ALL unrighteousness (1 John 1:9).

"For the law of the Spirit of life in Christ Jesus hath made me free from the law of sin and death. For what the law could not do in that it was weak through the flesh, God sending His own Son in the likeness of sinful flesh, and for sin, condemned sin in

the flesh, that the righteousness of the law might be fulfilled in us who walk not after [according to] flesh but after [according to] spirit" (Romans 8:1-4). There is no special spiritual power we need to walk spiritually. Notice that Paul says we already walk according to spirit rather than according to flesh if we are in Christ. There is no condemnation for us because the righteous requirement of the Law has been fulfilled.

"For they that are after [according to]flesh do mind [set their minds on] the things of flesh, but they that are after[live according to] spirit, the things of the Spirit. For to be carnally-minded is death, but to be spiritually-minded is life and peace. Because the carnal mind is enmity against God; for it is not subject to the law of God, neither indeed can be. So then, they that are in the flesh cannot please God" (Romans 8: 5-8).

We have become spiritually-minded. Because our citizenship is in heaven as members of the family of God, we know the truth that we are aliens and sojourners in this world. This life is not all there is. So we have the capacity to not worry about the things of this life, knowing that Christ will take care of those things as well as the future things in the world to come (see Matthew 6:33). This kind of thinking brings us life and peace rather than destruction and anxiety. Remember, He always does good; He makes all things work together for our good. ALL things, not just some! Carnal mindedness is simply a focus on this world's values rather than God's, which leads us to act in carnal ways rather than His ways.

"But ye [all of you] are not in flesh but in spirit, if so be that the Spirit of God dwell in you. Now if any man have not the Spirit of Christ, he is none of His. And if

Christ be in you, the body is dead because of sin, but the spirit is life because of righteousness. But if the Spirit of Him that raised up Jesus from the dead dwell in you, He that raised up Christ from the dead shall also quicken[give life to] your mortal bodies by His Spirit that dwelleth in you" (Romans 8:9-11).

The Holy Spirit dwells in all Christians; it is not necessary to experience repeated "fillings" of the Spirit to assure yourself that God is working in you. We are "in the Spirit" because the Holy Spirit of God dwells in us, and He will give life to our mortal bodies. That is eternal life, the life that never dies, the victory over all conceptions of death.

"And I, brethren, could not speak unto you as unto spiritual [people] but as unto carnal, even as unto babes in Christ. I have fed you with milk and not with meat [solid food]; for hitherto [until now] ye were not able to bear it, neither yet now are ye able; for ye are yet carnal. For whereas there is among you envying, and strife, and divisions, are ye not carnal and walk as men? For while one saith, 'I am of Paul,' and another, 'I am of Apollos,' are ye not carnal? Who then is Paul, and who is Apollos, but ministers by [through] whom ye believed, even as the Lord gave to every man?" (1 Corinthians 3:1-5).

Therefore, since all these things have been given to us, we focus on living as Jesus lived (1 John 2:6) which means sin has no more power over us.

"Let not sin therefore reign in your mortal body, that ye should obey it in the lusts thereof. Neither yield ye your members as instruments of unrighteousness unto sin, but yield yourselves unto God as those that are alive from the dead, and your members as instruments of righteousness unto God. For sin shall not have dominion over you, for ye are not under law but under grace.

What then? Shall we sin because we are not under law but under grace? God forbid! Know ye not that to whom ye yield yourselves slaves to obey, his slaves ye are to whom ye obey, whether of sin unto death, or of obedience unto righteousness? But God be thanked that ye were the slaves of sin, but ye have obeyed from the heart that form of doctrine which was delivered you. Being then made free from sin, you became slaves of righteousness.

I speak after the manner of men because of the infirmity [weakness] of your flesh. For as ye have yielded your members slaves to uncleanness, and to iniquity unto iniquity, even so now yield your members slaves to righteousness unto holiness" (Romans 6:12-19).

Slaves are required to obey their masters and we are freed from slavery to sin and have become slaves to righteousness. Sin need not be obeyed. We have the power to not sin (1 Corinthians 10:13) and certainly we have been empowered to live righteously. We sometimes do sin but we are convicted of it by the Holy Spirit who dwells in us, we confess it and are forgiven. But the basic general nature of our lives is righteous not sinful. We practice righteous lifestyles rather than sinful ones. We who are in Christ will not be condemned if we slip and commit one sin (1 John 1:9). WE ARE IN CHRIST. We cannot sin badly enough to change that situation. He has transferred us from the kingdom of darkness into His kingdom. He has already died for ALL sins. We do not want to sin; we do not practice sinful lifestyles. Stop putting yourselves into bondages. You have been freed from all bondage to sin, the devil, the world, even yourselves. WE ARE IN CHRIST.

It is most important that we do not fall into the propaganda of the world which identifies and confuses evil as good and good as evil. The Bible is our guide to identify the good and the evil, and it is there we recognize how we should judge these things. If the Word does not specify an action as good or bad, we look for principles and the revelation of God's nature to guide us. Just because the world accepts such things as couples living together before marriage or without marriage, does not mean that Christians can approve. There are many things in the world that are legal but not morally right according to the Word of God.

" For Christ is the end of the law for righteousness to everyone that believeth. So then faith cometh by hearing, and hearing by the word of God" (Romans 10:4, 17).

Let me also say at this point that faith comes by hearing the Word of God, which means that God has chosen the gospel as the avenue by which people will be saved. Faith comes by hearing the gospel, not by casting out demons or changing governments or any other activity. Not that those activities might not be good things too, but evangelism is not halted by demons or governments or opposition from people. Otherwise the gospel would have never moved from Jerusalem in the first place. The Christian Church would have never been able to grow, all Christians would have been killed, and the gospel light would have been extinguished. God is the one in charge of the spread of the Gospel and preaching is His tool for salvation.

Now, let's discuss a very important subject for Christian life: works. As we all claim to know, salvation comes by the grace of God. No person can earn salvation.

As Paul said **"And if by grace, then it is no more of works; otherwise grace is no more grace. But if it be of works, then is it no more grace; otherwise work is no more work"(Romans 11:6).**

But our problems tend to come after we have been saved. Then we think everything depends on us; how much we pray, how often we read the Word, how many ministries we volunteer for, how many church meetings we attend, and so on. It is almost as if God saves us and then disappears into the heavenlies, awaiting our performance. If we perform correctly, we get blessed. If we do not, then bad things happen. This notion is nothing but a load of rubbish.

Hear Paul's admonition to the Galatians about this very wicked idea. **" O foolish Galatians! Who hath bewitched you that ye should not obey the truth, before whose eyes Jesus Christ hath been evidently set forth crucified among you? This only would I learn of you: Received ye the Spirit by the works of the law, or by the hearing of faith? Are ye so foolish? Having begun in the Spirit, are ye now made perfect by the flesh? Have ye suffered so many things in vain—if it be yet in vain?   He therefore that ministereth to you the Spirit and worketh miracles among you, doeth He it by the works of the law, or by the hearing of faith?" (Galatians 3:1-5).**

We are indeed foolish if we think we have any power in ourselves to make things happen. Sorry but we do not heal nor save nor deliver anyone. God does all those things, according to His will, not according to ours. We must live by faith not by performance. Our Western cultural biases incline us to want to do something, to create a consistent formula that always works, an assembly line perspective that we can depend on to produce the same thing each time. That is NOT a Christian life.

Christianity is all about relationship, with God and with each other, not about production. We can pray all we want, sacrifice all we want, do all manner of religious things all we want, to no avail. We cannot force God to do things, we cannot persuade Him or coerce Him or manipulate Him in any way. In other words, we do not control life; He does.

We cooperate with His will and we have the great privilege to work with Him as He goes about His earthly work, but results do not depend on our performance of formula-based religious activity. All world religions pray, sing, make offerings, read "holy" writings, and such religious things. The difference is that we do these things as aspects of our relationship with a Person, Jesus Christ. We do not do them to be religious; we do them to honor God and help our ability to relate to Him. God does not need for us to inform Him of certain information; He is omniscient. He doesn't have an ego problem and need praise or worship. He doesn't need our human efforts to get things done; He is omnipotent.

He wants relationship with humans, hence Christ was incarnated and salvation was effected by Him in human form. We only need to do as He directs. He has chosen to work with and through us, in relationship, so we get the privilege to see Him work and participate with Him. So we learn to expect Him to do things; as we see Him work, our trust in Him grows. That is the theological point of all ministry. Atheists can be philanthropists. We work with God and in His name.

"I have planted, Apollos watered, but God gave the increase. So then neither is he that planteth

anything, neither he that watereth, but God that giveth increase. Now he that planteth and he that watereth are one, and every man shall receive his own reward according to his own labor. For we are laborers together with God; ye are God's husbandry, ye are God's building…

Every man's work shall be made manifest; for the Day shall declare it, because it shall be revealed by fire; and the fire shall try every man's work, of what sort it is. If any man's work abide which he hath built thereupon, he shall receive a reward. If any man's work shall be burned, he shall suffer loss; but he himself shall be saved, yet so as by fire. Know ye not that ye are the temple of God and that the Spirit of God dwelleth in you? If any man defile the temple of God, him shall God destroy. For the temple of God is holy, which temple ye are. Let no man deceive himself. If any man among you seemeth to be wise in this world let him become a fool that he may become wise" (1 Corinthians 3:6-9, 13-18).

"Whether, therefore ye eat or drink, or whatsoever ye do, do all to the glory of God. Give none offense, neither to the Jews nor to the Gentiles nor to the church of God, even as I please all men in all things, not seeking mine own profit, but the profit of many, that they may be saved" (1 Corinthians 10:31-33).

"But we have this treasure in earthen vessels, that the excellency of the power may be of God and not of us" (2 Corinthians 4:7). It is all about Him, not about us.

So, Paul said, "I beseech you therefore, brethren, by the mercies of God, that ye present your bodies a living sacrifice, holy, acceptable unto God, which is your reasonable service. 2 And be not conformed to this world, but be ye transformed by the renewing of

your mind, that ye may prove what is that good and acceptable and perfect will of God" (Romans 12:1-2).

Notice that the transforming comes by renewing the MIND. Christians need to learn things; we should be thinking people, not mindless spiritualists. Jesus expects us to believe that He has overcome the world, and we do not need to conform to worldliness (keep ourselves unstained by the world) but be transformed into witnesses who have overcome the world's power and temptations. We offer ourselves as sacrifices to God, rejecting the worldly measures of fame and power, available to do whatever He desires. **"For the kingdom of God is not meat and drink, but righteousness and peace and joy in the Holy Spirit... Let us therefore follow after the things which make for peace and things wherewith one may edify another" (Romans 14: 17, 19).**

There are a few specific issues of which Christians need to be aware. Paul commands, **"Let every soul be subject to the higher powers [governing authorities]. For there is no power but of God; the powers that be are ordained of God. Whosoever therefore resisteth the power resisteth the ordinance of God, and they that resist shall receive to themselves damnation. For rulers are not a terror to good works, but to the evil. Wilt thou then not be afraid of the power? Do that which is good, and thou shalt have praise of the same. For he is the minister of God to thee for good. But if thou do that which is evil, be afraid; for he beareth not the sword in vain; for he is the minister of God, a revenger to execute wrath upon him that doeth evil. Wherefore ye must needs be subject, not only for wrath but also for conscience sake. Because for this cause, pay ye tribute [taxes]also, for they are God's ministers attending continually upon this very**

thing. Render therefore to all their dues: tribute [taxes] to whom tribute is due, custom to whom custom, fear to whom fear, honor to whom honor" (Romans 13:1-7).

Let us understand that the concept of government is the idea of God, not the social contract, not convenience nor safety conceived by human society. Government's major role is protection of citizens from crime and wickedness. Citizens who obey the laws and live peaceably should not be interfered with by government. This idea was one of the major considerations of the Founding Fathers of the United States.

European governments coerced their citizens and forced them to follow certain procedures which inevitably enriched rulers but devalued common citizens. Socialism, Nazism, Totalitarianism, and Communism are all ideas that depend on coercion to force people to become all the same. Equality in this sense is the enemy of freedom. Free people will never all be equal and a society where everyone is equal in all things will never be free. Government, as conceived by God, was never meant to be coercive and oppressive but freeing so that society would be free and safe.

Paul's instruction also verifies that government bears and wields the sword, which means that crime must be punished and evil doers are the ones forced to be restrained from freedom. Even bad rulers should be treated with kindness and respect by Christians. We are the people who love, because God is love. We are the good citizens, treating our neighbors as we want to be treated. That does not mean we sit back and let evil people kill us or injure us or steal from us. Such people ought to be restricted, according to the will of God who placed government in the earth. The Ten Commandments say "Thou shall do no murder," not thou shalt not kill." Self defense is perfectly acceptable for Christians.

The apostle Peter confirms Paul's exhortations regarding the practice of good citizenship.

"Submit yourselves to every ordinance of man for the Lord's sake, whether it be to the king as supreme, or unto governors, as unto them that are sent by him for the punishment of evildoers and for the praise of them that do well. For so is the will of God, that with well-doing, ye may put to silence the ignorance of foolish men— and not using your liberty for a cloak of maliciousness, but as the bondservants of God. Honor all men. Love the brotherhood. Fear God. Honor the king" (1 Peter 2:13-17).

Giving seems to be a problem to many Christians though the Scripture should be very clear on the topic. The tithe of ten percent used in the Old Testament is not a requirement for New Testament believers but merely a guideline, a rule of thumb, a place to start. Malachi 3 indicates that blessings do flow toward the people of God as they recognize that they contribute to the work of ministry by giving a tithe and that otherwise they are robbing God of support for that ministry. But the apostle Paul also makes it clear that Christians should give cheerfully and generously, especially to those in need.

"But this I say: He which soweth sparingly shall reap also sparingly, and he which soweth bountifully shall reap also bountifully. Every man according as he purposeth in his heart so let him give, not grudgingly or of necessity; for God loveth a cheerful

giver. And God is able to make all grace abound toward you, that ye, always having all sufficiency in all things, may abound to every good work"(2 Corinthians 9:6-8).

We should have no needs since the Lord is our shepherd and He will provides for us in every way. That does not mean what one little girl said as she tried to quote the 23rd Psalm, "The Lord is my shepherd, I shall get what I want." Some of us have big "wants" that are not really good for us, and God will not give us more than we are capable of handling. Our lives should be models of contentment and trust, not the old worldly proverb that riches mean that God loves us more than others or we are more righteous and therefore more blessed than others. It is all about Him; not about us. Having more money or possessions than others is dangerous; we might fall into the trap of the world and live carnally, wreaking havoc in the lives of others and ourselves. We therefore possess things with care, aware that we are stewards of a gift from God, primarily to be used to bless the Church.

So Christians should give generously, to ministry and to the needs of others, without care for the percentages of income. Some rich people have a hard time even giving ten percent or giving regularly. If all Christians gave just the tithe, we could do much, much more for the spread of the gospel and meet the needs of the poor. But we must not be coercive or put people in bondage. Christ set us free and we should live that way.

"Stand fast therefore in the liberty wherewith Christ hath made us free, and be not entangled again with the yoke of bondage. Behold, I, Paul, say unto you that if ye be circumcised, Christ shall profit you nothing. For I testify again to every man that is

circumcised that he is a debtor to do the whole law. Christ is become of no effect unto you whosoever of you are justified by the law; ye are fallen from grace [turned away from grace]. For we through the Spirit wait for the hope of righteousness by faith. For in Christ Jesus neither circumcision availeth anything nor uncircumcision, but faith which worketh through love..."(Galatians 5:1-6, 16-18, 22-25).

Official doctrinal or religious rules do not mean more than faith working through love. So many Christians are simply Pharisees, following religious rules, rather than living in a love relationship with Christ. All that we are and all that we have, we received from God because of His grace, His generous favor. Not that we ever deserve anything good from Him but, because of Christ, God is just and gracious to give us even more than we ask or think. We get nothing from religious rules except the praise of men, which is ultimately useless and selfish.

"This I say then: Walk in the spirit [new regenerated nature], and ye shall not fulfill the lust of the flesh [fallen nature]. For the flesh lusteth against the spirit, and the spirit against the flesh; and these are contrary the one to the other, so that ye cannot do the things that ye would. But if ye be led of the spirit, ye are not under law... But the fruit of the Spirit is love, joy, peace, longsuffering, gentleness, goodness, faithfulness, meekness, self-control. Against such there is no law. And they that are Christ's have crucified the flesh with the affections [passions] and desires. If we live in the spirit, let us also walk in the spirit"(Galatians 5:16-18, 22-25).

Let's be sure we understand Paul's instruction here in Galatians. As a typical literary image, Paul contrasts two opposites here; spirit and flesh. By "spirit" he means spiritual or spiritually-minded, thinking about the things of God, godliness, rather than "flesh" which here means the carnal or fallen human desires and actions. So let's re-translate the passage: "Walk spiritually and you will not fulfill the desires of the fallen nature. For the fallen nature opposes the spiritual things of God, and the spiritual things oppose the things of the fallen nature. But if you are led by the spiritual things of God, you need no law to restrain your behavior. Indeed, the fruit or result of living spiritually is the manifestation of such godly qualities as love, joy, peace, . . . Against these behaviors and qualities there is no law needed. Those in Christ have made the fallen nature's passions and temptations powerless, so since we live spiritually, let us walk spiritually as well."

Equally, Paul instructs the Ephesians that they should **"I ... beseech you that ye walk worthy of the vocation [calling] wherewith ye are called, with all lowliness and meekness, with longsuffering, forbearing one another in love, endeavoring to keep the unity of the Spirit in the bond of peace..."** (Ephesians 4:1-3). **" This I say, therefore, and testify in the Lord, that ye henceforth walk not as other Gentiles walk, in the vanity of their minds... if so be that ye have heard Him and have been taught by Him, as the truth is in Jesus: that ye put off, concerning the former conversation [conduct], the old man which is corrupt according to the deceitful lusts, and be renewed in the spirit of your mind, and that ye put on the new man after God is created in righteousness and true holiness"** (Ephesians 4:17-24).
"Be ye therefore followers of God as dear children. And walk in love, as Christ also hath loved us and hath given Himself for us, an offering and a

sacrifice to God for a sweet-smelling savor... For ye were sometimes darkness, but now are ye light in the Lord. Walk as children of light (for the fruit of the spirit is in all goodness, and righteousness, and truth), proving what is acceptable unto the Lord. And have no fellowship with the unfruitful works of darkness, but rather reprove [rebuke] them. For it is a shame even to speak of those things which are done of them in secret. But all things that are reproved are made manifest by the light, for whatever doth make manifest is light. See then that ye walk circumspectly, not as fools but as wise, redeeming the time, because the days are evil" (Ephesians 5:1-2, 8-16, 17-21).

Spiritual Warfare

Nowhere in Scripture are humans ever called "spirit beings." Angels and demons are spirits. God is spirit. We are not called to become "spirits," which is a Platonic philosophical notion. We are special creations; humans which include a physical aspect that we cannot escape. Paul indicated that even at the resurrection our bodies will be changed, made to be spiritual bodies, which means bodies that will not perish anymore, like Jesus' body (see 1 Corinthians 15). As such, we humans are involved in the earth, as witnesses and ministers of Christ.

Nowhere are we told to enter into the spiritual world or to fight spiritual beings or to inhabit the spiritual world. God works with us here in the earth. Our spiritual warfare has only two dimensions: casting out demons who, by inhabiting some humans, bring physical and mental illness and destruction (Mark 16:15-18; Luke 9:1-2); and casting down imaginations and all thoughts that oppose the knowledge of God (2 Corinthians 10:5). There are no other examples or commandments that involve us in any other aspect of contact with demonic powers. The devil's fight against us is in the mind. He suggests actions that are bad for us and we either resist or accept them. We also can work to diminish or eliminate social ills, crime, disease, warfare, or other destructive forces in the world, all of which are the devil's inspiration. But he cannot physically assault us or directly attack us. If he could, he would have long ago.

Our responsibility is primarily to stand against his mental assaults and resist the temptations he suggests. We also pray for each other to be strong against his attacks on our faith, not directly on our bodies. And we do our best to reveal the truth that opposes his lies. That is the extent of our responsibilities. God has done or will do the rest.

The most famous passage regarding this issue is Ephesians 6:10-19. This text is greatly misunderstood and misinterpreted. Let's comment piece by piece. **"Finally, my brethren, be strong in the Lord and in the power of His might" (vs. 10)**. Note that the power is HIS might not ours. Now Paul uses a metaphor of the Roman soldier's armor which he uses twice before in other passages, though not as extensively.
" Put on the whole armor of God, that ye may be able to stand against the wiles of the devil"(vs. 11). Again the goal is to stand against the <u>tricks or deceptions</u> of the devil.
" For we wrestle [contend] not against flesh and blood, but against principalities, against powers, against the rulers of the darkness of this world, against spiritual wickedness in high places"(vs. 12). "Wrestle" is not the best picture here. The Greek word means "contend" or "oppose" and Paul's picture of the Roman soldier's armor indicates that (1) we are protected already, (2) we do not literally, physically fight

as the Roman soldier against a human foe, but (3) stand against the deceptions and schemes of the devil intended to keep us from faith in Christ.

"Wherefore take unto you the whole armor of God, that ye may be able to withstand in the evil day, and having done all, to stand. Stand therefore, having your loins girt about with truth, having on the breastplate of righteousness, and your feet shod with the preparation of the gospel of peace; above all, taking the shield of faith wherewith ye shall be able to quench all the fiery darts of the wicked. And take the helmet of salvation, and the sword of the Spirit, which is the word of God; praying always with all prayer and supplication in the spirit, and watching thereunto with all perseverance and supplication for all saints— and for me, that utterance may be given unto me, that I may open my mouth boldly to make known the mystery of the gospel..."(vs. 13-19).

Note that the pieces of armor are symbolic and represent aspects of our empowerment which we already experience through the Holy Spirit dwelling in us: Truth, Righteousness, the Gospel of Peace, Faith, Salvation, and the Word of God.

Truth defeats deception and lies;

Righteousness defeats wickedness and ungodliness;

The Gospel of Peace defeats the bad news of death, cynicism, defeatism, and hopelessness;

Faith defeats doubt, insecurity, and the idea that humans are here on earth by themselves as victims of cosmic random forces;

Salvation defeats the idea that after this life, there is nothing, that we are bound to sin and destruction and annihilation;

The Word of God defeats all other ideas, religions, efforts of humanity to solve all earthly problems, and every ungodly ethical rationalization. The only things we are told to do are (1) stand, and (2) pray for all the saints. Nothing is in this passage to indicate that we should try to cast out so-called "powerful territorial spirits" to free up the gospel for evangelism or engage in spirit battle in a spirit world in order to take over the earthly territory that supposedly belongs to the devil. The devil is already defeated by Christ. Jesus said ALL authority in heaven and earth belongs to Him (Matthew 28:18). No one has any more authority than He. He has the keys of death and the grave (Revelation 1:18). We have nothing to fear from our adversary, since Jesus is the king.

Flesh and Blood

In the Ephesians 6 passage, Paul mentions that we contend not with flesh and blood. The meaning is that we do not literally, with weapons, attack physical people as if we were in a physical war with them. But Paul does not restrict our spiritual warfare to demons but includes actions to thwart the efforts of people who are servants of the devil, wreaking havoc in society and on God's people.

Notice the following passages of Scripture:

"And it came to pass in Iconium that they went both together into the synagogue of the Jews, and so spake that a great multitude both of the Jews and of the Greeks believed. But the unbelieving Jews stirred up the Gentiles and made their minds evil affected against the brethren. Long time therefore abode they, speaking boldly in the Lord, which gave testimony unto the word of His grace, and granted signs and wonders to be done by their hands. But the multitude of the city was divided: and part held with the Jews, and part with the apostles. And when there was an assault made both of the Gentiles and also of

the Jews, with their rulers, to use them despitefully and to stone them, they were aware of it and fled unto Lystra and Derbe, cities of Lycaonia, and unto the region that lieth round about. And there they preached the gospel"(Acts 14:1-7). All of the conflict here was humans against humans, Jews against Christians, and the attempts of the believers to overcome the attacks by preaching the gospel and working miracles.

"... holding faith and a good conscience, which some having put away [rejected], concerning faith have made shipwreck, of whom are Hymenaeus and Alexander, whom I have delivered unto Satan that they may learn not to blaspheme"(1 Timothy 1:19-20). Paul here deliberately punished two people who blasphemed. If it were only some spirits who opposed him, Paul could have just cast them out. But this issue had to do with two men in need of discipline by the apostle.

"I exhort therefore that first of all supplications, prayers, intercessions, and giving of thanks be made for all men, for kings and for all that are in authority, that we may lead a quiet and peaceable life in all godliness and honesty" (1 Timothy 2:1-2). Paul's admonition is prayer for men, not prayers to cast out demons that make it difficult for Christians to live peacefully.

"This thou knowest, that all they which are in Asia be turned away from me, of whom are Phygellus and Hermogenes. The Lord give mercy unto the house of Onesiphorus, for he oft refreshed me, and was not ashamed of my chains..."(2 Timothy 1:15-16). Paul here criticizes and compliments men, not demons.

"But shun profane and vain babblings, for they will increase unto more ungodliness. And their word will eat as doth a canker. Of whom are Hymenaeus and Philetus, who concerning the truth, have erred saying that the resurrection is past already; and overthrow the faith of some… And the servant of the Lord must not strive [quarrel] but be gentle unto all men, apt to teach, patient, in meekness instructing those that oppose themselves, if God perhaps will give them repentance to the acknowledging of the truth, and that they may recover themselves out of the snare of the devil, who are taken captive by him at his will" (2 Timothy 2:16-18, 24-26).** Again, two men are judged here to have spread false teaching, and to have given their own lives to serve the devil by so doing, not an exhortation for the Church to go cast out demons. The servant of the Lord corrects <u>people</u> in opposition. We are accountable for our sins and errors; we can't blame it all on demons.

"Yea, and all that will live godly in Christ Jesus shall suffer persecution. But evil men and seducers shall wax [grow] worse and worse, deceiving and being deceived. But continue thou in the things which thou hast learned and hast been assured of, knowing of whom thou hast learned them…"(2 Timothy 3:12-14).

There are evil <u>men</u> who do bad things, who are deceived by the enemy and go about deceiving others – that's the plan of the devil, not literal, physical attacks on people. Christians are persecuted by <u>people</u>, who are encouraged by the devil and their own guilt of sin.

"I charge thee therefore before God and the Lord Jesus Christ, who shall judge the quick [living] and

the dead at His appearing and His kingdom: Preach the word! Be instant [ready] in season and out of season. Reprove, rebuke, exhort, with all longsuffering and doctrine. For the time will come when they will not endure sound doctrine, but after their own lusts, shall they heap to themselves teachers having itching ears; and they shall turn away their ears from the truth, and shall be turned to fables. But watch thou in all things, endure afflictions, do the work of an evangelist, make full proof of thy ministry... Alexander the coppersmith did me much evil. The Lord reward him according to his works. Of whom be thou aware of him also, for he hath greatly withstood our words. At my first defense no man stood with me, but all men forsook me. I pray God that it may not be laid to their charge" (2 Timothy 4:1-5, 14-16).

Notice again the references to <u>men</u>, some by name whom the Lord will punish, not a reference to some mighty demon that needed exorcism. The men must be opposed; the men will be punished; the men spread the false teaching. All the evil is inspired or encouraged by the devil but he does not literally come after and physically assault us. So when Paul mentions that we contend not against flesh and blood, he means that, unlike soldiers who literally strike and attack the flesh and blood of enemies, we contend against the inspiration, the lies and falsehoods brought by the devil, which is lived out in humans on the earth. But we do not literally fight them in the usual physical sense.

Principalities and Powers
In another aspect of the Ephesians 6 passage, the phrase "principalities and powers" appears. We usually understand that to mean some hierarchy of powerful demons. However note other passages that use the same

phrase "principalities and powers" (which literally means "rulers and authorities" in Greek):

"**For I am persuaded that neither death nor life, nor angels nor principalities nor powers, nor things present nor things to come…**" (Romans 8:38).

"**… far above all principality and power and might and dominion, and every name that is named, not only in this world but also in that which is to come**" (Ephesians 1:21).

"**… to the intent that now unto the principalities and powers in heavenly [high]places might be known by the church the manifold wisdom of God**" (Ephesians 3:10).

"**For we do wrestle [oppose, contend] not against flesh and blood, but against principalities, against powers, against the rulers of the darkness of this world, against spiritual wickedness in high places…**" (Ephesians 6:12).

"**He [Jesus]is the image of the invisible God, the firstborn of every creature. For by Him were all things created that are in heaven and that are in earth, visible and invisible, whether they be thrones or dominions or principalities or powers. All things were created through Him and for Him**" (Colossians 1:15-16).

"**… and ye are complete in Him, which is the head of all principality and power. …blotting out the handwriting of ordinances that were against us, which were contrary to us. And took it out of the way, nailing it to His cross. And having spoiled [disarmed] principalities and powers, He made a show [public** spectacle] of them openly, triumphing over them in it" (Colossians 2: 10, 14-15).

"Put them in mind [remind them] to be subject to principalities and powers (rulers and authorities), to obey magistrates, to be ready for every good work..." (Titus 3:1).

Some of these references must be understood as human rulers, certainly Titus 3. "Heavenly places" can also mean "high places" and thus refer to humans. But the major point is that, if there are different levels of demons, all of them, as well as all human powers, have been submitted to Christ, who is the head of all rulers and authorities. We have not been given a commission to rid the world of mighty demons.

Remember there is no power in heaven or earth or anywhere else that is remotely comparable to God's power. Our Savior and Lord is head over all such beings, and He takes care of us in this world and all worlds. There is no need for us to fear anything. **"Be careful [anxious] for nothing but in everything by prayer and supplication with thanksgiving let your requests be made known unto God, and the peace of God which passeth all understanding shall keep [guard] your hearts and minds through Christ Jesus;"** (Philippians 4:6). **"Peace I leave with you, my peace I give unto you, not as the world giveth, give I unto you. Let not your heart be troubled, neither let it be afraid"** (John 14:27).

Social Aspects of Christian Life
There is a social aspect to Christian living that involves community reputation and defending the faith of Christ to the world. Evangelism, socio-political values

and issues, materialism, consumerism, social justice, and community welfare are just a few of the public issues that Christianity must address in the 21st century. To do so, we need to recognize some foundational biblical principles that can guide us.

"If ye then be risen with Christ, seek those things which are above, where Christ sitteth on the right hand of God. Set your affection [mind, heart] on things above, not on things on the earth. For ye are dead, and your life is hid with Christ in God. When Christ who is our life shall appear, then shall ye also appear with Him in glory" (Colossians 3:1-4).

This passage points out the location of our ultimate reality, a heavenly life. Our values here on earth must reflect the values of God; our concerns and interests must reflect His. I believe that when we arrive in the heavenly life, so many of our earthly worries and concerns will be so irrelevant that they will not even come to mind. Even in our eternal existence, everything about us is bound up in Christ. He is our life; when He appears in glory we will as well, with Him.

Since that is the case, we should **"Mortify [put to death] therefore your members which are upon the earth: fornication, uncleanness, inordinate affection [passion], evil desire, and covetousness, which is idolatry"(Colossians 3:5).** The reference to put to death means "make of no effect, no power." In other words, make them irrelevant and powerless to affect us. If we realize that they are powerless to force us, and that they are so irrelevant and valueless, then the tempting aspect, the attractiveness of them, disappears. We've outgrown them, like a person outgrows the sandbox which was so wonderful in childhood.

"Put on therefore, as the elect of God, holy and beloved, tender mercies, kindness, humility, meekness, longsuffering; forbearing one another, and forgiving one another, if any man has a quarrel [complaint] against any; even as Christ forgave you, so you also do ye"(Colossians 3:12-13). The term "put on" simply means "do this as a part of who you are."

" And above all these things put on love, which is the bond of perfection. And let the peace of God rule in your hearts, to the which also ye are called in one body; and be ye thankful. Let the word of Christ dwell in you richly in all wisdom, teaching and admonishing one another in psalms and hymns and spiritual songs, singing with grace in your hearts to the Lord. And whatsoever ye do in word or deed, do all in the name of the Lord Jesus, giving thanks to God the Father through Him... And whatsoever ye do, do it heartily, as to the Lord and not unto men, knowing that from the Lord you shall receive the reward of the inheritance; for ye serve the Lord Christ"(Colossians 3:14-17, 23-24).

Evangelism
"Walk in wisdom toward them that are without [outside], redeeming the time. Let your speech be always with grace, seasoned with salt, that ye may know how ye ought to answer every man" (Colossians 4:5-6).   Evangelism requires some wisdom.

The old American assembly-line methodology, all Christians presenting the gospel the same way to everyone, will not be welcomed in the 21st century. Paul told us in Colossians that our speech should be seasoned with salt and grace, knowing how to answer questions about our faith. Some Christians use the excuse that they are not theologians, not trained in seminary, and therefore can't witness to other people. This is no excuse. The Lord does not expect every Christians to be able to walk up to strangers on the streets and present a sermon. But we should not be stupid and uninformed either. We should be knowledgeable about the Bible; we should learn to talk to non-Christians; we should know our theology well enough to help people who seek answers to the big questions of life.

Christians have not accepted this responsibility and have not learned their faith. Churches need to push heavily the education ministries and teach people their theology. Christian colleges should make classes available to members of local churches, not to increase their student numbers but as a service to the body of Christ. Christians need to know biblical theology and know how to answer questions that non-Christians may ask.

As well, we need to realize that each of us has personal social agendas, based on many different values and feelings. Since the world tends not to function by logic or common sense, we find ourselves fighting others, even brothers and sisters in Christ, over whose agendas will dictate public issues. If we all knew and accepted the basic nature of God and His values and principles revealed in Scripture, there would be fewer differences among us in these areas.

The apostle Paul sums up the social ministry of the local church with this admonition:
"Now we exhort you, brethren, warn them that are unruly, comfort the fainthearted, support the weak, be patient toward all men. See that none render evil for evil unto any man, but ever follow that which is good both among yourselves and to all men. Prove

all things; hold fast that which is good. Abstain from every appearance of evil" (1 Thess. 5:14-15, 21-22). "For the grace of God that bringeth salvation hath appeared to all men, teaching us that, denying ungodliness and worldly lusts, we should live soberly, righteously, and godly in this present world, looking for that blessed hope and the glorious appearing of the great God and our Savior Jesus Christ, who gave Himself for us, that He might redeem us from all iniquity and purify unto Himself a peculiar people [His own special people], zealous of good works. These things speak, and exhort, and rebuke with all authority. Let no man despise thee.

Put them in mind [remind them] to be subject to principalities and powers, to obey magistrates, to be ready to every good work, to speak evil of no man, to be peaceable, gentle, showing all humility unto all men" (Titus 2:11—3:2).

One of the major concepts revealed to us in Scripture about social ministry is the idea of the Body of Christ. The Church is not just a meeting place for like-minded people, nor is it primarily for fellowship of the organization. We are the body of Christ in the earth. We function this way by His sovereign choice. Christ is the head of the Church, the one in charge of His church. It is His church, not ours. When begin to think that the church is ours, we've just created a social organization, a human institution. A real church is a local representation of the universal Church, led by Christ, walking in love, and demonstrating that love by acts of service to the community.

The Lord provided "gifts" in the form of ministers who teach and mold us for our own ministries. **"And He gave some apostles, and some prophets, and some evangelists, and some pastors and teachers, for the** perfecting [completing, equipping] of the saints for the work of ministry, for the edifying of the body of Christ, till we all come to the unity of the faith and of the knowledge of the Son of God, to a perfect [complete] man, unto the measure of the stature of the fullness of Christ; that we henceforth be no more children, tossed to and fro and carried about with every wind of doctrine, by the sleight [trickery] of men, in the cunning craftiness whereby they lie in wait to deceive, but, speaking the truth in love, may grow up into Him in all things which is the head— even Christ— from whom the whole body, fitly joined together and compacted by that which every joint supplieth, according to the effectual working in the measure of every part maketh increase of the body unto the edifying of itself in love" (Ephesians 4:1-3, 11-17).

Notice that these ministers are given by God to equip us to do ministry, not to do all ministry themselves. They are intended to diminish their own roles and increase everyone else's ministries. Any ministry that seeks to insulate and elevate itself errs. We help each other grow in ministry so that eventually we all "come to the unity of the faith and of the knowledge of the Son of God," not so that one person can become highly exalted and be put on a pedestal by grateful church members.

We should all learn proper theology so that we are not deceived by false teachers. Each person in the Body has a role, a ministry, without which the Body suffers. Everyone is needed; no one is to be excluded, no ministry neglected (see 1 Corinthians 12:12-26). We need every church, every Christian denomination and tradition. None of us has all the knowledge or strength. We are a Body not Lone Rangers, operating all on our own. We cannot reject other Christians and be a healthy local body. All the "lists" of manifestations of the Holy Spirit (spiritual gifts) are simply samples; they are not exhaustive. So if you do not see your 'gift' listed in 1 Corinthians 12 or Romans 12, remember that they are examples and that there are many other ways the Holy Spirit manifests Himself.

Christians respond to the situations of the world in several ways. First, there are some things we simply flee. Not every possible temptation affects everyone. We may not ever think to rob the bank on the corner but pornography may be a harder test. Drug addiction may not be considered a pleasant possibility to us but drinking alcohol may be hard for us to control. We realize that temptations must be considered pleasant for them to be tempting. If they were seen for the misery that they produce, we would be less likely to fall prey to them. Know your weaknesses and which ungodly actions are real temptations for you. Develop a strategy to deal with them. The best time to decide to get up when the alarm clock rings is the night before, not at the time it actually rings. The bed is too comfortable then.

Contemplate which things tempt you. Think of strategic ways to resist them, long before they ever arrive. Prepare your mind to follow the strategic plan when the temptation appears. Mentally practice over and over again what you'll do when the temptation comes so that you can develop more of a reflex response to the temptation. God will always provide us a way out of every temptation so that we may escape them (1 Cor. 10:13). Use your plan.

Paul instructs his protégé, Timothy, about some of these problems. "**. . . strife about words. . . envy, strife, railings, evil surmising, perverse disputings of men** of corrupt minds and destitute of the truth, supposing that gain is godliness; from such withdraw thyself. But godliness with contentment is great gain. . . . For the love of money is a root of all evil. But thou, O man of God, flee these things and follow after righteousness, godliness, faith, love, patience, gentleness. Fight the good fight of faith, lay hold on eternal life, where unto thou art also called and hast confessed the good confession in the presence of many witnesses" (1 Timothy 6:4-12).

In our age of history, we tend to define success in terms of numbers: church members, people who are saved in a crusade, the number of countries preached in, finances received, large homes, new cars, expensive clothing, and so on. We so easily fall into the traps Paul mentioned to Timothy. Perhaps these traps are the cause of so many ministries falling into sin and disgrace. Our focus is not on righteous living but on achievement that competes with the success of non-Christians in our culture.

Equally, we are required to demonstrate our faith and service by our concern for people in trouble. The non-Christian world elevates Mother Theresa as the best example of Christianity. Why? Because she ministered to the sick, hurt, and hopeless without monetary gain for herself. She sought no fame or fortune. She demonstrated selflessness, sacrifice, and genuine love for all people. James strongly recommended that same approach to life for Christians, as evidence of their salvation and commitment to Jesus.

"What doth it profit, my brethren, though a man say he hath faith and have not works? Can faith save him? If a brother or sister be naked and destitute of daily food, and one of you say unto them,

'Depart in peace, be ye warmed and filled,' notwithstanding ye give them not those things which are needful to the body, what doth it profit? Even so faith, if it hath not works, is dead being alone. Yes, a man may say, 'Thou hast faith, and I have works.' Show me thy faith without thy works, and I will show thee my faith by my works. Thou believest that there is one God. Thou doest well. The demons also believe—and tremble! But wilt thou know, O foolish man, that faith without works is dead?" (James 2:14-20).

The essence of James' doctrine is that, since all people act according to their beliefs, Christian faith must be seen by our actions. Intellectual assent to the idea that God exists is not the same as a personal relationship with Christ and a new birth, which changes our hearts and minds, resulting in a life full of the fruit of the Spirit.

"Grace and peace be multiplied unto you through the knowledge of God and of Jesus our Lord, according as His divine power hath given unto us all things that pertain unto life and godliness, through the knowledge of Him that hath called us to glory and virtue, whereby are given unto us exceedingly great and precious promises, that by these ye might be partakers of the divine nature, having escaped the corruption that is in the world through lust" (2 Peter 1:2-4).

"And hereby we do know that we know Him, if we keep His commandments. He that saith, 'I know Him' and keepeth not His commandments, is a liar, and the truth is not in him. But whoso keepeth His word, in him verily is the love of God perfected. Hereby know that we are in Him. He that saith he abideth in Him ought himself also so to walk even as

He walked… And now, little children, abide in Him, that when He shallappear, we may have confidence and not be ashamed before Him at His coming. If ye know that He is righteous, ye know that everyone that doeth righteousness is born of Him" (1 John 2:3-6, 28-29).

"In this the children of God are manifest and the children of the devil: Whosoever doeth not righteousness is not of God, neither he that loveth not his brother"(1 John 3:10).

Some people think that such a life is too difficult for them to achieve, and they are right. We can only live by the fruit of the Spirit if the Spirit lives in us, and we surrender the control of our lives to Him. The more we use our own human strength to try to do all the right things we think God wants, the more failure we will experience. It's like pushing a car through the streets. You could possibly move it some but what a difference when we turn the ignition key and allow the motor to propel the vehicle. The more we resist the guidance and power of the Holy Spirit, we more frustrating and fruitless our Christian life becomes. Get out of the way and allow the Spirit to move you. How?

We first must read and understand the Scriptures, then be in no hurry to make things happen the way we want them. Listen more in prayer rather than talk all the time. It is God's job to communicate to us, not our job to drag some word out of Him. He lets us know things when we need to hear them, not before. If you pray, and don't hear anything, then wait until you do. God will not be late. Often when the answer to our prayers is NO, we have been given direction, not rebuke. If this way is not the way, then there must be another way. Pay attention; don't get mad. **"Humble yourselves therefore under** the mighty hand of God, that He may exalt you in due time, casting all your care upon Him, for He careth for you" (1 Peter 5:6-7).

Walking in Love

Most Christians have changed hearts that usually care about people who experience difficulties or suffering. We tend to give to charities generously and pitch in to help the needy. Our problems come when we encounter difficult people or those who treat us unkindly. We forget or don't realize that the love of God in us requires a response that is different from the expectations of the world. We can yield to our old ways of dealing with these situations and become unkind, short-tempered, selfish, and unconcerned.

Walking in love often means remembering the real nature of love. We need to love when the person is not good, when people don't treat us well, when we are being cheated and mistreated. That does not mean we cannot insist on proper treatment or make sure the right is done. But our attitude must be one that mirrors 1 Corinthians 13. As well, we need to be more sensitive to the problems, fears, insecurities, and anxieties of the other person. Sometimes we may have to correct or discipline another person, a child or an employee, but we must do so with skill, patience, fairness, kindness, and truth. We certainly can get angry at times, but we must not "take it out" on another person. Better to be calm and perceptive, which may enlighten us about the reality of the situation and give us better approaches to dealing with them.

"Love suffereth long and is kind, love envieth not, love vaunteth [elevates] not itself, is not puffed up. Love doth not behave itself unseemly, seeketh not her own, is not easily provoked, thinketh no evil

[of others], rejoiceth not in iniquity but rejoiceth in the truth. Love beareth all things, believeth all things, hopeth all things, and endureth all things" (1 Corinthian 13:4-7).

"No man hath seen God at any time. If we love one another, God dwelleth in us, and His love is been perfected in us. Hereby know we that we dwell in Him, and He in us, because He hath given us of His Spirit. And we have seen and do testify that the Father sent the Son to be the Savior of the world. Whosoever shall confess that Jesus is the Son of God, God dwelleth in him, and he in God. And we have known and believed the love that God hath for us. God is love, and he that dwelleth in love dwelleth in God, and God in him.

Herein is our love made perfect that we may have boldness in the day of judgment; because as He is, so are we in this world. There is no fear in love; but perfect love casteth out fear, because fear hath torment. He that feareth is not made perfect in love. We love Him because He first loved us. If a man say, 'I love God,' and hateth his brother, he is a liar; for he that loveth not his brother whom he hath seen, how can he love God whom he hath not seen? And this commandment have we from Him: that he who loveth God must love his brother also" (1 John 4:12-21).

Love also involves keeping the commandments of God, not that they are requirements for salvation or righteous standing before God, since Jesus has paid for all of that. We should love His commandments as they are reflections of His nature and character. We should love doing things His way rather than the way of the world.

"For this is the love of God, that we keep His commandments. And His commandments are not grievous [burdensome]... And we know that we are of God, and the whole world lieth in wickedness. And we know that the Son of God is come and hath given us an understanding, that we may know Him that is true; and we are in Him that is true, even in His Son Jesus Christ. This is the true God and eternal life" (1 John 5:3, 19-20).

His commandments are always best, always right, always good, though we may not think so at the time. Lean not on our own understanding but in all our ways acknowledge Him, go to Him, hear Him, follow Him (see Proverbs 3:6-8). He will not lead us astray; He will not desert us; He will not treat us badly. He is faithful and trustworthy, so trust Him.

"Now thanks be unto God which always causeth us to triumph in Christ, and maketh manifest the savor [fragrance] of His knowledge by us in every place" (2 Corinthians 2:14). We will always be victorious because He leads us. We will not come up short. We will not, in the end, say that we failed, because He will make us come out right, **"...being confident of this very thing, that He which hath begun a good work in you will perform [complete] it until the day of Jesus Christ..." (Philippians 1:6).**

CONCLUSION

We have learned that God is so much more than we have been taught or imagined. He is always with us; we are always in His presence; He always hears our prayers. He always does good; He always does the best thing for us. We can trust Him with everything. He can handle any and all problems. He is the Master Weaver, who weaves all the incidents of our lives into a tapestry of life made just for us. Paul's incarceration in Philippi, though momentarily painful for him, resulted in the salvation of the jailor and his family as well as the spread of the gospel in that area (Acts 16:22-34).

Even our mistakes and problems get woven into the tapestry so that the best comes to us. He makes all things work together for our good. We can depend on Him. We can expect Him to work in every situation so that the best happens for us, even as Joseph told his brothers, "But as for you, ye thought evil against me, but God meant it unto good" (Genesis 48:20). God extravagantly blesses us, more than we ask or think or deserve, not with mere necessities for existence but with joy in serving Him and living for Him. He has all the power; no power can compete with Him. He always does what He wills; He takes care of us and thwarts our enemies, within His purposes to do us good and always causes us to triumph.

Jesus has done everything necessary to bring us salvation and eternal life with Him. He is our salvation, sanctification, justification, glorification, and anything else involved in establishing and maintaining a right relationship with God. We are in Him and, because of that situation, we live in a right relationship with God. There is no condemnation for us; we are God's children and heirs of Christ, made fit to live in eternity with Him.

We are safe in His hands; no one can remove us from Him, not even ourselves. We are His ambassadors, extolling His virtues and glorious Person to the world. Christianity is our relationship with Him, not a set of religious rituals or rules. We can trust Him to finish His work with us and come again to establish a new earth in which we will fellowship with Him and all Christians.

The Holy Spirit is a Person—God. He has come to help us along the way in our earthly journey. So we are not alone, and not victims subject to random cosmic forces. We do not have any tools to minister; we are the tools and the Holy Spirit does the ministry through us. He is the gift; He is the power. We are the privileged children who get to participate in His work. He is always working in the Church, and we need every Christian, every denomination, every local church, to complete the Body of Christ, whose head is Jesus. It is His job to communicate to us, not ours to drag some message out of. If we need to know, He will tell us. Our relationship is not based on our performance.

The Christian life is righteousness, peace, and joy in the Holy Spirit, not performance of religious rules and rituals. Our faith is in a Person—Jesus Christ. The Holy Spirit in us makes us capable of resisting temptation (1 Corinthians 10:13) and our major task is to minister to those in need and keep ourselves unstained by worldliness (purity). We take an active role in speaking the truth to the world, emulating the virtues of Jesus, being good citizens, and representing the ways and character of God.

In all that, the Holy Spirit has enabled us by relying on Him, who is the power. We should simply know God as He is revealed in Scripture and go about the business to which He calls us, in every field of endeavor, to demonstrate to the world that He loves all people. It is not our job to perform intensive, complex religious activities in order to receive blessings or to obtain mystical magical powers. The pedestal is not our place to stand, but His. We focus our lives on Him!

Index of Scriptures

NOTES

NOTES

NOTES

NOTES

NOTES

NOTES